Perfect Pictures

To My Soul-Sister Janine — I thank God for sharing the love God, because he led me to you. You are my touch-stone and my dear, dear friend. Thank you for all your love and for allowing me to be apart of your life. I love you. Your Soul-Sister

Perfect Pictures

Christy Whitman

GMA Publishing

Newburgh, Indiana

ISBN: 1-59268-038-0

GMA Publishing
Newburgh, Indiana

GMAPublishing.com
Check out our website
GMA is a global publishing company
Our books are available and distributed around the world and can be found on the internet at Amazon, Barnes and Noble and any major bookseller.

GMAPublishing@aol.com

Cover By: Cecilia Brendel
Manuscript Assistant: John Beanblossom

Printed in the United States of America

An inspirational book for

those who like it

"Perfect"

I dedicate this book to all of my spiritual teachers and authors that have given their gifts and talents into the universe for me to embody to help transform my life. This book is guided by spirit.

Contents:

Acknowledgments

I am so grateful to the many spirits who, throughout my life, have given me the love and support I needed to help make my own dreams come true:

To my family:

My father, Frank Valesh, for always being such a great provider. For always teaching me to do my best, and for always letting me be free to experience my own life. I cherish precious moments with you.

My mom, Inez Valesh, for teaching me about perfect pictures, and for always wanting the best for me. I love our new friendship and I am very proud to be your daughter.

My sister, Theresa Valesh, through your life and your death you taught me what is most important; Love. Thank you for all that you went through, so I didn't. You were my first spiritual teacher, and an incredible sister. I will see you in my dreams.

My husband, Mike Whitman, you have taught me about loyalty, commitment, honest, integrity, and unconditional love.

You are truly my best friend and my life partner. I am a better person because of you. Thank you for the gift of laughter.

My stepson, Ryan Whitman, you are such a bright light in this world. You have taught me to be flexible and helped me release my control pictures. You are a lucky strike extra.

My mother and father in-law, Dixie and Bill Whitman, for accepting me, and loving me unconditionally into your family since day one. For being my friend, and for creating the most amazing man.

My grandparents, Ron and Isabelle Pacioni, for always making family come first, special moments, and whisker tickles.

My Godmother, Maryanne Wiles, for always seeing me as a precious child, and a beautiful spirit. Words can never express what you mean to me and how you have brightened my life.

To my spiritual teachers:

Melanie Flores, for teaching me Light Body and for opening my heart.

Rebecca Grado, for empowering me as a woman, and freeing me from my darkness. You are my soul sister.

Dr. James Golden, for getting me in touch with the Goddess inside of me. Thank you for all your honesty and teaching me to stand in my truth.

Dr. Andrea Golden, for helping me realize my passion and let go of what was not serving me. Thank you for being an incredible incarnation of Spirit, and a role model of a strong spiritual warrior.

Terry Cole-Whittaker, for showing me how to live with passion, and helping me realize the truth of who I am.

Barbara DeAngelis, for showing me how love really works through your teachings. You were my first personal growth teacher.

Introduction

I wrote this book because of the amazing growth I was experiencing in my life. I really tapped into an incredible spiritual awareness and principles that were altering my experience. Issues that had bound me for years were transforming, and my life was becoming so beautiful and so abundant.

By being willing to open to spirit, I was able to realize places in my life that did not serve me. If I wanted to attain my topmost desires, I needed to release that which no longer served me, and so I did. Attending classes through my church I was able to take a deeper look at my life and issues that were making my life unpleasant. Through this awareness I realized that I had what I refer to as "Perfect Pictures". Having this awareness I was able to accept where it no longer served me. I diligently worked at changing those pictures, and then I released it to spirit, and became a much happier person. I realized that I was not the only person that had to experience life and situations the way I wanted it, or else there was suffering. I was given a vision while in meditation to create this book that will help others to transform their lives the way I have transformed mine.

This book is a gift from Spirit.

1

Pictures

PERFECTION IS AN ILLUSION. When we have unrealistic expectations of ourselves, and others, we will experience suffering in our lives. We are left feeling that what we do, who we are, and what we have is never good enough. Trying to achieve perfection is like trying to hit a moving target. When will we ever be satisfied? We do have the power to create greatness in our lives. It is our right to make our dreams come true. We can learn how to create the most beautiful dream, while being detached from that which causes us to suffer. Our lives can then manifest into a series of wonderful experiences that go beyond our wildest dreams.

Each person has images in one's mind. The mind holds these images of what the past, present, and future look like. Similar to when you are at the beach and you take a picture with your camera. After the film is developed, or now with digital cameras-immediately, there is a picture. The mind holds the same type of pictures. When you think of your past experience of being at a beach a mental picture comes up. If I mentioned a carnival, most people would be able to remember a time at a carnival. They would remember everything that was significant of that experience. That is the picture. For those people that have never been to a carnival, they would try to use their imagination to create a mental picture of what a carnival might look like.

We hold pictures in our minds based on what the present looks like. The interpretation of the picture that we are looking at can be filtered through our emotions, logic, past wounds, etc. I'm sure there have been many experiences where you and another person were looking at the same thing, together sharing the same experience. The interpretation of the experience could be completely different based on other people's life experiences. Think about two people that witnessed a car accident. Based on where the two people were standing, the experience and description of the accident could be completely different even though it was the same car accident.

This happens many times during romantic relationships. Something was said from one person, and the other person interprets it in an entirely different way, possibly causing an argument or hurt feelings. We all have different pictures in our minds based on our personalities, past experiences, past wounds, etc. The way we filter and process information is different from person to person. We all live in our own minds.

Just as there are pictures of the past and present, there are also pictures that people have about the future. The mind holds an image of what the future or a situation should look like based on their beliefs, dreams, desires, goals, etc. These images held in the mind, or what I refer to as pictures, are what starts the creative process in the universe, good or bad. There is a principle in the universe that is "Your thoughts create your reality". What you picture in your mind as something positive, or negative, will manifest.

This is how we create Heaven or Hell on Earth. Heaven or Hell is not a destination, but a state of consciousness. As defined by Webster's dictionary, "Heaven is a spiritual state of everlasting communion with God; a place or condition of utmost happiness". You will notice it does not include, "after you die."

Many great books have been written on the power of visualization. Visualization has great creative power.

If your mind can conceive it, you can achieve it.

The power of visualization, imaging, or having 'pictures' is a mental activity consisting of vividly picturing, in your conscious mind, your desires or goals. Holding that picture in your mind over and over has the capacity to have it sink into your unconscious mind, where it then creates your reality. This is a powerful process, coupled with faith in Spirit, as your co-creator of your goals and desires. Being vigilant with holding these pictures in your mind, praying, and having gratitude that the pictures will manifest can be used as a very powerful tool in your life.

My life has changed considerably by working not only with my conscious mind, but also the unconscious mind.

My Pom Pon Line Visualization

It was freshman orientation at my high school. The pom and cheer line came out to show us their stuff. Being a cheerleader always appealed to me. I tried out in 7th and 8th grade, but did not make it either time. The cheerleaders did a cheer, and then the Pom Pon girls danced for the audience. I was awestruck. I wanted to be dancing with those girls with every part of my being. I told my mom that I was going to be a Pom girl. I knew it in my heart and soul. There was nothing that was going to stop me. I visualized myself constantly as a Pom girl in the uniforms, wearing the pom pons on my shoes and, carrying them in my hands. I would imagine what it would be like to dance for the school at assemblies. Every way I could imagine it, I did. I went out of my way to talk to the pom girls to gather information on what they had to do to join and make the squad. Many of them were very generous with the information.

The end of my freshman year I tried out and I made the squad. I did not only visualize myself doing it, but I worked very hard to do the best that I could do to make it, and I did. I remember having many conversations with God about my desires. There wasn't a fountain that I didn't pass where I would throw in a penny and make a wish. My wish came true.

Be, then Do, and you will Have.

I have many more stories of how I visualized events and desires that came true for me. I have heard many stories about other people that had the same experiences. It is incredibly powerful and it works.

My pictures in my mind help me visualize and create my pom pon experience, as well as many other beautiful memories and many desires. As I mentioned earlier that the images we hold in our minds create either Heaven or Hell, happiness or suffering, joy or pain. My perfect pictures created both for me.

2

Perfect Pictures

ATTENDING CLASSES, CHURCH, LISTENING TO tapes, praying, meditating, journaling, reciting affirmations and treatments helped me realize that I was suffering in my life, because of the expectations I put on myself and others. I was very judgmental about myself and other people. One of the ministers at the church, who is one of my greatest spiritual teachers, spoke one day about judgment. He said that the reason that we judge comes from the desire to have someone change something, based on what you hold in your mind to be what should be, instead of what is. If the person, place, or thing is different from that picture in your mind and you cannot accept it as it is, you desire to make it fit to the picture by changing it, and then you judge.

If you have acceptance and love for others for who and what they are, there is no desire to change them, and therefore no need to judge. This is also true for the self. If you love yourself unconditionally, you will not constantly find fault with yourself, and therefore judge yourself. For example, if a person is very overweight and you in your mind think that this person needs to be thinner, you want them to change, you then judge them. Instead of seeing the beauty of the person, you truly miss the person, your mind has judgment, and the heart is then closed.

I really started paying attention to when I judged other people. I would then ask myself "What is it that I want this person to change?" I would then practice acceptance of the person. I know my mom was one I judged on a daily basis, based on the desire to make her act or behave differently. Once I accepted my mom for who she was, there was no judgment, and our relationship improved significantly.

We judge ourselves worse than we judge others. The unrealistic expectations that we have about other people are harmful. It is even more harmful to our own selves. When we judge ourselves, we blame ourselves, and then find ourselves guilty, and then feel the need to punish ourselves. I realized that I had some major issues in judging myself that did not serve me.

My Weight Issues

My mom had "perfect pictures" on everything. The clothes, nails, complexion, make-up, weight, and hair all had to be perfect. She always looks the best she possibly can. There was always just "one thing" or "one problem" with a given situation, because it was not "perfect". For example, my husband and I gave my parents a dinner boat trip when they were visiting us on vacation. The boat was really terrific. It sat four people and we sat up in front of the boat with a nice bottle of champagne. The owner of the boat rowed us down the Sacramento River, while cooking us a great dinner. It was wonderful. The four of us sat there in a beautiful surrounding, we were enjoying champagne, and each other's company. After some champagne we needed to use the restroom. There was no restroom on the boat. We needed to pull over and walk on the shore and find a spot. I thought it was so funny.

Until the day I die I will never forget this experience. My mom is such a classy lady, and to see her in that light was nothing more than a bonding experience. I held it as a precious moment forever. She held it as it was a great gift, but there was only one problem: no bathrooms. She made this the focus of the trip and missed out on how special it was. It was not perfect, because there were no bathrooms. She actually sat there and tried to think how the man could put bathrooms on his boat. She missed it by her perfect pictures. It is the follies in life that make moments like these memorable.

At some point in my life, I made a decision and embodied the agreement that I had to be perfect, and so adopted the "perfect pictures". It did serve me and still does, because I always try to look the best I can. Where this has always been harmful is in the area of my weight. I have always wanted to look better than I actually did. I would obsess and be compulsive about my weight, what I ate, food, etc. I always held an image in my head that I was overweight.

What you contemplate, you become.

I have struggled with my weight my whole life, even though I was never truly overweight. Many women fight with bad body images and it is so self-defeating. Many women truly hate their bodies, and if asked, "What is the one thing you love about your body?" a large majority of women would have a difficult time finding that part. Why are we never satisfied with our own bodies? Why do we constantly put ourselves down? Why do we always want to look like someone else other than ourselves? What would happen if we learned to love ourselves?

I realized I had a huge problem when I looked back at my honeymoon pictures. I looked so great. My body was so strong, lean and tiny. I remember what I said to my husband when we were on the honeymoon, and how I felt. I told him that I was going to really hit it hard when we returned home so that I could loose more weight. I was a size 2 and in the best shape I had been in years. I sincerely did not feel that I looked as good as I actually did. It was never good enough. I was a size 4, and wanted to be a size 2. I became a size 2 and then wanted to be a size 0. I then wanted to look like Janet Jackson instead of myself. I sabotaged myself and started gaining weight.

My Realization With My Friend

I was spending time with a girlfriend of mine and we were discussing how she and her husband had been together for over 10 years. She was saying that it was getting challenging being creative sexually. I was offering her some creative suggestions on how to spice it up. I mentioned doing a strip show and dance for her husband. She shamefully looked down when I mentioned this and said, "That would not work". She then told me that her husband, who is a wonderful man, was a perfectionist and was not happy with her body. She is a very beautiful and attractive woman. She has always had what we laugh and say is the "Italian butt". But, he knew that going in. He was missing on truly loving his wife and accepting her unconditionally based on the pictures that he held in his mind. He had "perfect pictures". This conversation obviously disturbed me, being newly married. I then realized that because my body wasn't perfect in my mind, I was not doing these creative things for my husband. In that moment I realized that I also had perfect pictures. In many spiritual teachings it is taught that others reflect back to you things about yourself, good or bad.

The universe is set up as a reflection of what is going on inside of you. People in your life will mirror parts of yourself for you to look at and bring to a higher light. The universe will bring people and circumstances into your life that will cause issues to come up in order to be healed. I had such a reaction to this that I went inside myself to find out what the reaction was about. These "perfect pictures" were causing me a great deal of suffering. I was never satisfied with anything, including myself. I never felt that anything was ever good enough.

In a creative living class I mentioned my obsession with my weight, my perfect pictures, and how I wanted to create a better body. The minister that I mentioned earlier made me stand up and asked everyone in the group if they thought I had a problem with weight. This was really embarrassing for me. It also brought up a lot of my fears of being rejected based on what my body looked like. Nobody in the group said yes. I was relieved, but in my mind I felt that I knew I looked good, but I wanted to look better. To ask these people their opinions shouldn't matter. I knew the way I wanted to look, and it wasn't how I looked at that moment. I felt their ideas of what thin was, was different than mine. I then made up an excuse that "I get it, but..." and he firmly spoke "No, you don't get it, and that is the problem". He then said, "I don't believe you have a career that requires you to look like a model on the cover of a magazine". I told him "No, but if I didn't strive for a perfect body, what would my body look like then?" He helped me realize that by having perfect pictures, it allowed me to be conscious of my body and weight. I feared that by releasing my perfect pictures I would become apathetic and let myself go. He asked me "If you accept and love yourself and your body, do you really think that would happen?"

In that moment I realized that the pictures I had been holding in my mind were unrealistic and never good enough, based on what I thought my body "should" look like. As I did a mind treatment I wept for all of the negative energy I was giving to myself each time I touched my leg, or looked in the mirror. In that moment I made a decision to release my perfect pictures. I made an agreement to love myself, while being conscious of creating my ideal.

There is nothing wrong with having desires and achieving goals, such as having the form that you want for your body, abundance, wealth, happiness, a specific job etc. This is our right as humans to desire the topmost, and co-create with God to achieve all of our dreams. The universe is set up so that we all create our happiness and abundance. Some people really know how to step into this creative process, and constantly work on themselves or their goals in order to achieve them. There are universal laws that have been taught by many spiritual writers, and religions that teach the steps to have success in this universe.

Desiring the topmost is great. Where this can pose a problem is when the pictures in one's mind have to be perfect. It needs to be exactly how you picture it, or else there is dissatisfaction and a great deal of suffering. I know, for I have suffered with "perfect pictures". I have now learned acceptance and detachment. I have learned to set goals, do the work in attaining those goals, but surrendering to the final outcome. Webster's dictionary defines perfect as "being entirely without fault or defect: flawless" or "corresponding to an ideal standard or abstract concept". Webster defines pictures as "a mental image". Having perfect pictures of my body or anything else for that matter, sets myself up for unrealistic expectations which then leads to suffering. The spirit that is within me is "entirely without fault or defect". The mind would make us believe that everything outside of the spirit could possibly be flawless and it is our mental image that keeps us in trying to achieve that unrealistic standard.

Growth is why we are here. Instead of us falling asleep in our lives we are to awaken to a bigger consciousness. Many people live their lives by waking up, going to work, coming home, going to sleep and doing it all over again. This robotic type of existence is not what is intended for our lives. Each one of us has a power within us to go beyond greatness. That power within each one of us is Spirit, and is truly the only thing in the Universe that is perfect.

3.

Sub-personalities

I BECAME AWARE OF SUB-PERSONALITIES within myself when I started meditating. I took a very intense series of meditation classes called "Awakening Your Light Body", which helped me evolve my sub-personalities. A Sub-personality is a part of your personality, such as the part of you that fears, worries, likes to embrace life, desires perfection, and so on. These sub-personalities within each and every person are always trying to do the best they know how for the individual. Many of these sub-personalities were created as a survival technique for when we where children and we did not know how to cope with different situations in our lives. When we grow and evolve, these sub-personalities need to transform as well.

The meditation journeys that were guided on the tapes assisted me in giving various parts of my personality a new vision of who I was. As I integrated and evolved all of the sub-personalities, I created immediate and very powerful changes in my feelings and thoughts. Having the awareness of these sub-personalities, that no longer served me in the best way that they know how, was the first step. Letting them go was the second step.

Some may call these sub-personalities habit energy such as anger. Within our ego we have many sub-personalities that make up the whole. These can include personalities or habit energies that are anger, sadness, joyous, childlike, mischievous, impeccable, and so on. They are trying there best, but many do not work or serve us any more. The good news is that they can be evolved. They can be changed.

My Anger Sub-Personality

I grew up with a father that really had a lot of anger issues. He handled a great deal in his life from a place of anger. I adopted those anger habit energies and truly thought that I was unable to change them. The excuse that was given in the family to make the anger explosions tolerable or excusable was that we were Italian and Italian's have hot tempers. I bought into that agreement and belief and made it ok for me to have my own explosions and temper tantrums. It was said that it was something that was out of our control. Just as the Irish drink, Italians yell.

We need to be careful of the false labels that we put on ourselves. If we say, "I am shy. I am not athletic. I am Italian and therefore have a temper" we are defining ourselves and each time we think, "I am (fill in the blank)" we are reinforcing that belief. Those beliefs will create our reality. We are then creating the conditions for our life experience. Dr. Wayne Dyer said, "You create your thoughts. Your thoughts create your intentions. Your intentions create your reality." We control the conditions for our lives. We can create or change any type of personality or trait we want. We have that power within us. It is our choice, because we are the ones that control our own thoughts. If you don't control your own mind, who does? We can replace those old definitions of ourselves with new positive and empowering ways of being by making the choice to do it. We learn to tell ourselves a different story.

I had been on a spiritual quest for many years. There had been times when I really welcomed in the darkness so that I could bring it to the light. There have been other times that my ego and personality took hold and ran the show for a while. When I was truly in my heart, and out of my ego, my anger did not surface as much. What I later learned is that when you don't take anything personally, there is nothing to be angry about. I did finally realize that my anger issues were not serving me, or those that shared their lives with me. It had become a place of suffering in my life. What could I do though? I was an Italian. I was powerless to its control over me. Or was I? My husband never bought into the belief that I had a temper because I was Italian. He thought it was a cop out and an excuse for me not to change and evolve. He was right. Some of my closest girlfriends are Italian, and they do not have tempers. My grandparents were Italian and they did not have tempers. Not all Italians have tempers. It was a belief I embodied and I was the one in control of changing the belief.

When I started attending The Redding Church of Religious Science, I was faced with the knowledge that we all can create what ever we want in our lives. It is our creation. It is our blank canvas and we are the artists to create the most beautiful life painting if we choose. One of the ministers spoke about habit energies and I related it to the sub-personalities that I had previously worked with. I took responsibility for my life and realized that I could change this anger habit because it was no longer serving me, if it ever did at all. It wasn't something I just said "O.k. I realize this and now it is gone". This was energy or a sub-personality that was deep in my conscious and sub-conscious and took work to change. I had the power to change it. I just needed to know how and put it to work. The realization that I had the power to change anything in my life that I desired was very liberating to me. I was no longer controlled by my darkness. I became a sponge and very committed to my spiritual path. I attended church, retreats, seminars, and classes to be fully absorbed in the right way of thinking. I learned I had a choice in what I thought about, and I better make the right choice because thoughts are things. Thoughts have a creative process that can either manifest as good or bad. This is why it is so important to be impeccable with your word. I wanted the best in life. Where I was experiencing pain in my life was because I created that pain with previous thoughts. Many people think that our outer circumstances determine our inner. But it is really the inner that determines the outer.

As within, so without.

For example, great majorities of people look outside of themselves for happiness. Many people think that by finding a perfect man or woman they will then find happiness. If the happiness is not generated from the inside, and a conscious choice has not been made to be happy, the greatest person in the world could come into your life and you will not experience happiness. Many people think I will be happy when I find the right partner, lose twenty pounds, when my kids are married and successful, have my own business, I redecorate my living room, I finally get the promotion, when I get a new car and so on. Happiness is a choice that comes from within that can be created from a higher source. That source has unlimited happiness for us to tap into. You and I are one with that unlimited source of happiness. It comes from within.

I know for myself, my relationship with my husband is always more beautiful when I am in connection with Spirit, my higher self. I am filled up in God's love and the love is unending. God has an unlimited supply. When I look to my husband to fill me up, it does not work. He has a lot of love to give, but God is the one with abundant supply. When I am filled with my own love, Mike is able to give to me much more freely. When I look to him as my happiness, I am always disappointed. Not because he as a person is incapable, it is just how the Universe works. When I look at Mike as my source, he can feel that pressure and it pushes him away. It then feels like rejection to me. I created what I was defending against. Whatever he does, it is never good enough. He can't give me enough affection or love to fill me up entirely, so I am still left feeling empty and abandoned. The happiness, love, and, joy we feel can't come from another person. It comes from within.

It has been said that more women today cheat on their husbands than do men. I can understand that if a woman feels empty and is not in touch with her higher self, she would look outside of herself to be filled up. If she looks to her husband and he is unable to fill her, and another man should show her attention, it could be very seductive to think, she could be filled up by someone else. This is a lie. So many people are looking outside of themselves for happiness, only to find disappointment.

The divorce rate is now sixty-five percent. Sixty-five percent of marriages end in divorce. Why? Most people go into marriage looking for something. When the other person doesn't give them what they are searching for, they try to find it somewhere else. Look within, and look up and the fulfillment will be there.

I choose a consciousness of Heaven, not Hell

So where did the perfect pictures come into play? In every area of my life I experienced perfect pictures. Some of the pictures had positive results. Other perfect pictures caused a lot of suffering in my life.

It has been taught by many spiritual leaders that we choose our parents before we take a body, and I certainly chose mine. My mom had perfect pictures, and I learned and embodied them. I accepted my perfect pictures wholeheartedly. I used them for all the great things they helped me create, and all the times where they made me suffer. As I mentioned earlier, my mom was always concerned with the outside appearances. In her attempt to show our family love, and wanting our happiness, she wanted everything to be perfect, including us.

My sister would always get the questions while on the phone with my mom: Are your nails short? You know you ought to get fake nails. What about your skin? Do you have any boils? You know you ought to go to a dermatologist. Are you wearing your hair curly or straight? You look much better with it straight. The conversations went this way until she felt that she covered everything she needed to do in order to help her become "perfect". If something was not perfect, you must fix it. It felt like disapproval. It felt hurtful. She was just trying to do her best in what she perceived as helping us. My sister never bought into the pictures that she needed to change her outer appearance. She however was a perfectionist about everyone and everything else. She tried, but it did not fit her image. She never truly learned to love herself. I, on the other hand did take on the perfect pictures regarding myself and my appearance, and they did serve me up to a point.

Mother and Her Weight

One thing I remember about my childhood, and it still happens today is my mom saying "I'm going to hit it hard on Monday". Meaning that come that magical Monday she was going to start a diet, only to fail a few days later, or blow it on the weekend. I said those words on my honeymoon. At this point I did not realize, or had become conscious of this issue or how it had affected my life.

Other people mirror back to us what we need to look at in ourselves.

My mom would check herself in the mirror and just be disgusted by what she saw. My mom is a very beautiful woman and has never been overweight. She has never had a super-model body, but who ever told her she needed to? Her own perfect pictures that she held in her mind. The way she spoke was that this was unacceptable and something needed to be done. She had perfect pictures of what she needed to look like, all the while throwing negative thoughts and energy at her body. I adopted this as well, and finally took a stand and said: NO MORE!

All of my sub-personalities, even my perfect pictures, served me. My hands were always manicured, as well as my toes. My clothes were always sharp and attractive. I always wore the best-branded clothes. My hair and make-up were always perfect. My skin was beautiful. And then there was my weight. Looking back, I had a darling figure. I was not skinny. I have always been short with strong muscles. I was always trying to make my body what it wasn't, and I suffered greatly. The more I obsessed and was compulsive about my weight, the more weight I would gain. I even started smoking when I was 16 years old to try to control my weight. I only had a weight problem in my mind, as many of us do.

We view models and actors and actresses on television or the movies and we compare ourselves to them. We then beat ourselves up because we don't look the way they do. If we are short we want to be tall. If we are brunette we want to be blonde, if we have curly hair, we want straight. Instead of appreciating our own beauty and loving the characteristics that we have, we want to be like someone else. We are never satisfied. I remember the day that I realized that I was short and stocky. I realized I was always trying to have long lean legs. No matter how lean and strong my legs were, I wanted them to be different. That was a very freeing day to realize and accept my body for the frame that I was given. To reinforce that acceptance of my frame, my husband came into my life and admired my body. He is not attracted to tall, skinny women. He is attracted to women that are short and have shape to their bodies. This was so amazing to me because I always thought that every man just wanted a tall thin woman. When we accept and love ourselves, the universe will mirror those conditions back to us.

Jenny McCarthy was on the Rosie O'Donnell show when she was becoming popular because of the show "Singled Out". What struck me and stood out in my mind about this show was Rosie had a poster of Jenny. Jenny was so humble and really wanted younger girls to understand that she really was not that perfect like in the poster. She started drawing on the poster of where she had a big pimple. She then drew around the area of her flat stomach and said she was bloated on this day because of her period. She marked up the whole poster until she showed what she really looked like on that day. She explained that the poster was touched up and made her look perfect. I gained respect for her, because she was trying to convey to younger girls that there is no perfection. Perfection is an illusion.

I remember being a size 2 on my honeymoon, looking very sexy in my bathing suit and new tropical clothes. I told my husband that I wanted to loose weight. That was the "I'm going to hit it hard" conversation. I seriously did not feel good about myself. I felt like I looked fat. I now am a size 4 and feel better about my body than I ever have. Before when my perfect pictures did not serve me, I could have been a minus 4 and still not be satisfied with what I saw in the mirror.

The quest for perfection was a learned attitude and behavior. I learned this through family, friends, and society. I realized that not only for my own sake, but also for the sake of my unborn children, I needed to transform this agreement with myself. I did not want to teach my children how to suffer. I want to teach them how to love and accept themselves, while always trying to achieve being the best that they can be. Once I became aware of my own perfect pictures, I started noticing other people around me struggling with their own image of perfection.

My Husband's Pictures

My husband has an amazing physique. His body reminds me of the statue of David created my Michael Angelo that resides in Italy. He is perfectly proportioned and is very sexy. I have witnessed him looking at himself in the mirror and pinching what I refer to as skin on his stomach, because he does not have any fat. He does the same disgusting look to himself as my mom did to herself, and I did to myself. He then would beat himself up for not working out, or eating "perfectly", and then feel badly about himself. What does this sub-personality serve in him, other than to cause great and unneeded suffering in his life? It helps him be conscientious about his body so that he is conscious about working out and eating healthy. That is the positive purpose of his perfect pictures. However, there are other ways that he could ensure he has a healthy lifestyle, and learn how to release the self-mutilation. Being uncomfortable is a good emotion as it can propel a person into change if change is needed. If a person stays stuck in what is making them uncomfortable, such as their weight, it can cause a great deal of suffering. We have the power to make great changes in our lives. We can take the appropriate steps, and in addition, release our attachments to the outcomes.

When we are dissatisfied with areas in our own life, it is up to us to take the appropriate steps to change and grow. Where we do not have power is in other people's perceptions and opinions of ourselves. If we are doing our best and our own mate has perfect pictures of what we should look like, act like, or behave like, we have to allow them to work through their own perfect pictures. In the case of my girlfriend and her husband that has perfect pictures, she is left feeling that she is not good enough. No matter how beautiful she looks, he is dissatisfied. This can be very hurtful. She is being validated for her body, and not her spirit. She is not her body. She is a beautiful spirit soul. When her husband is in his own perfection images of what she should look like, he is missing the true essence of who she is. He is truly missing her beauty and her perfection.

What sub-personalities are within you?

1.

2.

3.

4.

5.

Which of these sub-personalities need to be evolved to allow you to have self-respect, self-love, and self-approval?

1.

2.

3.

4.

5.

Are you willing to commit to evolving these sub-personalities to serve you in a better way?

As I mentioned, our sub-personalities do serve us the best way they know how. Because of my "perfect pictures" I was able to join the pom pon line. I was voted Sweetheart Attendant my sophomore year of high school. My senior year I was the Pom Captain, was voted most congenial, and also was voted and awarded the Homecoming Queen. My desires then led me to ASU for College. My new pictures were then to become a career woman. I remember telling my sister that I wanted to have a different colored suit for every day of the week.

I did.

My pictures all came true. I was 23, a very successful sales person living in Chicago. My career was on its way and it was the way I pictured it. I remember being an outsider looking at my life and thinking that I had it made. I lived with my best friend in a great apartment on the North-side of Chicago. I had a great career, my ideal body, and a good amount of friends, freedom, and money. But inside I was very lost and unhappy. I felt very disconnected. I was missing something. I found it when I moved to California. I found my spirituality.

4

You Have The Power

I WAS VERY HAPPY TO learn that it was ok for me to receive those things that I desired. What I did learn that enlightened me, and changed my whole life, was my awareness of my attachments to things. That is what perfect pictures is all about. The attachments to our pictures of what something should be, and not being happy until it turns out to meet the picture. Abundance is our right. God wants us to have all the best that is alignment with our Highest Good. It was ok for me to want to create the form of my body to look a certain way. It was great to try to do those things that led to the form I wanted to create such as eating well and exercising. What was not acceptable was any place in my mind, where I did not love myself. Any place that I held myself in a less than loving way. I had to give up every bit of self-hate, self-dislike, and self-disapproval. I also had to be connected to a source higher than myself to help me in this process. I had to know that as a creation of God, I was already perfect.

This change happened by having the desire to attain the form of my body be a size 2, and holding the belief that I would. I asked Spirit to help me create my form. I was also willing to release any place in my mind that would create the opposite effect.

When I would look in the mirror I would love and appreciate those parts of my body that I loved. I concentrated on my upper body and my abdominals. I validated how good I looked, but also held the vision of my size 2 frame that I was creating. Because I loved my body and told myself how great I looked, my subconscious, which is a very powerful part of our psyche, helped create the form. I also released the obsessive need for food, because I was being filled by spirit and loving thoughts. I used the following affirmations daily.

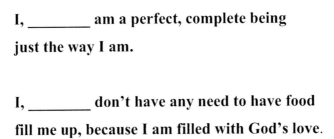

I, _____ am a perfect, complete being just the way I am.

I, _____ don't have any need to have food fill me up, because I am filled with God's love.

I also changed the beliefs that I held about myself, and certain foods. Tony Robbins in his <u>Get The Edge</u> program discusses that there are two controlling forces that direct our lives. Those two forces are pain or pleasure. He explained that everything we do in our lives is driven by our need to avoid pain and our desire to gain pleasure. In order for us to achieve what we want in our lives, we have to figure out what is stopping us. I had to dig deep and figure out what beliefs I was holding that kept me from achieving my ideal body, while in the same act loving myself and my body just the way it was.

What this used to look like from a very unhealthy mind was I would look in the mirror and focus completely on all the parts of myself that I wanted to change. I would literally grab the back of my legs and throw anger and negative thoughts about that section of my body. I would say to myself that I needed to be stricter on what I ate and really limit myself. I have a sub-personality that is a rebel and does not like to be told what to do. When I tell her she can't have something, that something is the first thing she wants. I would then tell myself that I was "starting" again tomorrow and then binge for the rest of the day, because I had to get it in while I could. I was about to deny myself every favorite food that I could, so stock up. Does this sound familiar?

I focus on progress, not perfection!

Perfection is an illusion.

What we contemplate, we become.

When you focus your attention on the positives you create more positives. Focus on the negatives and you manifest more negatives in your experience.

Terry's Perfect Pictures

Terry was one that suffered from the desire to have everything perfect. You bet when he created something it was unbelievable. But getting through the creation he was absolutely attached to having it perfect. This caused much suffering for him and those involved in his life. I was the recipient of many of those perfect occasions. If something did not go as planned, or the way he thought they ought to, he became hard to be around. His disposition was very unpleasant, critical, and judgmental. I remember one occasion when we were decorating the house for Christmas. I was in such a joyful, happy place. We decorated the entire house with lights and Christmas paraphernalia. I wanted to decorate the tree. I was listening to music, having the time of my life. He came back into the room and totally criticized how I had put the lights on the tree. He said I did it wrong and that it needed to be done a different way, the right way. What the heck was the "right" way? The lights looked beautiful. I thought somehow I don't think Christmas was supposed to be like that. My joy was no longer there. He mirrored perfectionism to me, and I later realized that I suffered the same way he did because of those pictures.

As I mentioned, you have the power. Self-reflection and self-realization is a very powerful process that many people can't experience because there is too much fear holding them back. Many people choose not to look at what is causing suffering, maybe because they don't know that they have the power to change.

The Day I Discovered I Could Change My Anger Habits

I looked deep inside and realized that I had the power to change my temper and anger habit energy. I knew it would take work on my part, but it was worth it to stop the suffering.

I purchased the book "Anger", by Thich Nhat Hanh. In the book he discusses what the anger is and that paying attention to the anger and analyzing the anger is an important place to start. The book also discussed not only how to get in touch with it, but how to transform it. I took the teachings from the book and applied it in my own life. To read about the teachings is one thing, but to practice is how one's life will transform. One can read all about an orange, the way it looks, feels, the texture, and the way it tastes. But if you have never actually tasted an orange, you have not truly experienced it. This is similar to achieving a goal. If you make a goal that is great, but in order to achieve the goal you need to take the steps that will lead toward its attainment. You need to take action.

I told my mom of my new discovery and apologized to her, as she was the recipient of many of my blow-ups. I told her it was no longer an energy I wanted to cultivate in my life. My mind was similar to a garden. There are beautiful plants and vegetables that get planted like beautiful thoughts. There are also weeds that have come up without our knowledge of how they got there. If you do not take out the dead weeds, the new growth of the good harvest will not grow. This was an energy that was in my mind, body and emotions and needed to be pulled out like a bad weed. It may grow back, but if I keep pulling it out and stop watering it will eventually die. Many therapist feel that the anger inside needs to be expressed and should be released by throwing pillows or hitting a punching bag. This may work for some people. It just cultivated more anger inside of me. I was watering the seed of anger. I felt it worked better for me to pull the weed out. My mom was very pleased to hear of my discovery.

She explained to my father what I had realized about myself. Both of us knew that I had learned the anger energy from my dad. When she told him of the self-discovery that I had and what I wanted to change, he honestly told her that he had no idea where I had gotten such a bad habit. We were both in amazement.

He truly did not realize that he has anger issues. He did not remember all the times in which he blew up. There are more people out there that are unwilling to look at their imperfections then individuals who want to improve themselves.

The fact that you are reading these pages says you are searching for a better life. You are a person that is willing to look at and change that which does not serve you. You want to increase the quality of the life you have. In that search, some of that which does not serve you, or is not for your highest good will fade from your life.

Are you ready to release that which does not serve you?

Are you willing to allow the "dark" parts to come up in order to come out?

What needs to fade from you life in order to be the person you desire, or to create the life you want?

1.

2.

3.

4.

Once you have realized and become aware of things that hold you back in your life, the second thing to do is recognize that you do have the power to change. This power is within you and it comes from the source of all that is. That source and supply is God, Spirit, Higher Self, True Self, or Infinite Spirit. Call this power whatever helps you feel connected, it doesn't matter. It is the connection with this power that will have great changes in life. I know it has in mine.

Tina Turner

A story that greatly affected my life was the Tina Turner story. Here was an incredibly talented woman that was caught in a very unhealthy and abusive marriage. She was able to tap into the power of the universe and found the power within her to see how her life was not working. She then made the changes that she needed to be a happier person. These changes did not happen over night. She had to work at her self, her spirituality, and have faith and trust in a power greater than herself.

She found the power of Buddhism and chanting. There are many great tools that can help a person gain power over their lives or things that they want to change.

Terry Cole-Whittaker, one of my favorite spiritual teachers, wrote in her book "What You Think of Me is None of My

Business" that each person needs to accept certain truths about our selves. There are five truths. Knowing these truths has changed my life. Her book helped change my life.

1. You are already a complete person, with nothing missing. God made us already complete.

2. You are a creative being. Our nature is to always be creating good or bad.

3. You create from your beliefs about yourself, life in general, and God.

4. You have made decisions that used to be conscious about yourself, others, and life that are now unconscious and direct your decisions and ultimately determine the quality of your life.

5. The universe is totally cooperative and supportive. It says yes to both the good and bad ideas, even if the ideas will destroy you.

This information empowered me. It also made me really pay attention to my thoughts. If it was true that our words have creative energy and is the power that we have to create, we need to pay attention to what we think, say, and do. If I truly wanted to live a joyous life, free from suffering I needed to become a witness to my thoughts. Eastern religions speak of this witness and paying attention to what the mind is saying.

Paying attention to the witness allows you to free yourself from your mind. Listen to the voice in your head as often as possible. Pay attention to repetitive thought patterns. When you hear a thought pattern that goes against yourself, or what you are trying to create in your life, change it. Replace the old thoughts with new thoughts. You have the power to change your thoughts. It is your mind. You control it. Paying attention and being present in the moment has great power for change.

The mind or the ego will try to overtake you. The ego cries loud and hard before it dies. I found myself purchasing a new home. It was our dream home. It was quite a bit more money than we currently paid. Everything that led up to purchasing the home and selling ours was effortless. Effortlessness is always a sign to me if something is to be for my highest. If there is struggle and I try to make it be, I need to step back and realize that it is not happening for a good reason. When my husband and I went to sign the loan papers for the new house, I had all sort of fears. It was a very strange thing, because I do not fear money. I never have and I never will give money my power. My belief is that money works for me. So here I was having all these fear thoughts. I did a prosperity treatment. I did a treatment about releasing my fears and doubts. It helped, as it always does, but my ego was really trying to win this time. My mind had a very powerful hold on me. I finally had to relax into the present moment and ask myself, "Do I have everything I need right here, right now? The answer was yes. I always do. "Is there any problem that I have in the now?" No. Your mind will try to convince you that there are things to fear. Be in the present moment and all that is left is consciousness. Have present moment awareness, and the fear subsides. When all else fails, take each moment and surrender into what is.

5.

Putting the Power Into Action

I ATTENDED A SEMINAR THAT Terry Cole-Whittaker was conducting at the church. The information she was sharing with the group was very informative. What really intrigued me about Terry is the passion that she had for life. I wanted that type of passion in my life. I purchased a workbook from her on generating wealth. This workbook turned out to be one of the greatest purchases I ever made.

She had made the point that you need to get really clear about what you want to create in your life, and then write it down. I already knew the power of writing things down, for that is how I created my husband.

My Perfect Man

After I had broke off an engagement to be married, a great friend of mine told me to get clear about what I do want in a mate. I knew from all of my past experiences, what I did not want. She said really stretch and write down all the characteristics on a sheet of paper and then tuck the paper away. I was very creative and wrote down every characteristic that I desired in a man. I had my previous therapist tell me that my list was unrealistic and my expectations were too high. One of my other friends read the list and said, "Yeah, if you find him, ask him if he has a brother". Both of them felt that my list was unrealistic. I took the paper with hope and tucked it away. After a couple of weeks of dating my husband, we were involved in a great conversation. In that moment I realized how many great qualities he possessed. I then realized that I had saved the piece of paper that had all the qualities that I wanted in a partner. I went into my drawer and proceeded to read every quality on that paper. My perfect man was sitting right in front of me. He had every characteristic on my list. I believed and had faith in the universe.

Funny thing is, I never wrote down on my list that the person couldn't have been married before, or had a child from a previous marriage. I was speaking to a co-worker one day about the type of guy I would like to meet. I told him that three things were out. He couldn't have been married before, had any children, or work for the same company as me. That co-worker told me that I was really limiting myself and could miss out on a wonderful person. I thought of my dear friend who had been married previously, and has a son. I thought if anyone met her, and decided not to be with her because of her past, they really would miss out on a really incredible person. A week later I met Mike. In this situation I did have perfect pictures. Before this talk with my co-worker I would not have realized the consequences of my limitations. I would have not been given the beautiful gift of Mike's heart, and the abundance of love from Ryan, Mike's son. I am grateful that I did not suffer because of those perfect pictures. I could not be more blessed to have them both in my life.

At the seminar Terry had us write down some of our desires and goals. I wrote down all my desires, which most of them have already manifested. I also wrote down three goals, which were achieved. She spoke about the importance of goals and the most important aspect was bringing God into those goals. I did just that.

What are your goals? What are your desires?

Have complete faith and trust that God wants us to be happy, successful, and prosperous. The whole universe is set up for us to achieve our topmost desires. It is up to each person to learn about themselves, Spirit, and the universal laws.

What do you want to achieve in your lifetime?

What does success look like to you?

What do you intend to achieve and who do you want to become?

These questions were hard for me to answer when the little me was looking at the material things in life that would bring me happiness, or I thought would bring me happiness. When the real me, the big me, the higher me became the captain of my ship I found my passions and achieved my goals. The change in consciousness to being one with God, and working for God, changed my life.

When I took this seminar from Terry I was somewhat happy. I felt blessed in life. I was not passionate about my life's work, nor did I realize I had a life's work. My big picture was working for the company I worked for as a pharmaceutical rep. I did want to create a new company, because my energy did not match with the one I currently worked for. One of my goals was to find my perfect career. I found it. One of the ways in which Terry suggested to build prosperity was to recite success mantras many times every day. This was to work with the sub-conscious mind, which is very important to turn into an ally. There were also mind treatments for success. Mind treatment is a spiritual practice that I learned while attending the church. I can't even begin to explain the amazing power behind prayer and treatment. You will have to experience it for yourself. I have given instructions on how to do your own treatments, as well as treatments you can start with in your life today.

At the seminar and in the workbook she had us sign a "Declaration of Wealth". This was a treatment stating that I believed in the source of my supply as God and nothing else. No organization, person, place or thing is the source of my supply. Since this day my inner and outer world has dramatically changed. One of the treatments was "Manifesting you Desires". You would read your goals and desires daily, at least three times a day, and then read the treatment. This took dedication and practice. Just as if you want to change something about your health, you need to be compliant with the treatments given to you by your physician. If you are typically not a compliant person, you have the power to change that. She had said these are the steps that you need to take to manifest what you want in life. I worked those steps daily.

In the "Manifesting your Desires" treatment there was a sentence that said "All that which is not for my highest good now fades from me and I no longer desire it". Two weeks later I was asked to resign from my company.

Creating a New Job

What an ego blow to be asked to resign from a position. I had always been successful at every job I had, and was always recognized as a leader in my company. At the time I was asked to resign, I was the number one representative in my district.

Because I had my faith I was able to find comfort in knowing that I would create something far better, and I did. The company I worked for was very ego-based. The way in which they wanted me to sell was not my style. I had always been successful in every sales position, because I build great relationships with my customers, not because I was a hard, aggressive closer. I truly felt that I could not be myself. When I tried, I would be asked to change. I had very low energy and no passion for my work. This job clearly was not in my highest good. I needed to destroy it so I could create something that was for my highest good.

I spent three months off of work, doing my part looking for work, interviewing, and applying for positions. What these three months off of work made me realize is who I truly am. I am not my job. I am not my body, my thoughts, my actions, my behaviors, my house, or my relationships. I am Spirit. I am one with God. I am like a ray from the sun, or a wave from the ocean. I am connected and apart of something so much bigger than myself, or my idea of myself. I went through so much growth during those three months that I am grateful that I left the job suddenly. My faith in Spirit was very strong, but after the experience, it was unwavering. I did my success mantras every day:

God is my Source and Supply.

God is my Protector and Maintainer.

There is nothing to worry about ever again.

I was amazed that money kept coming to me. I was asked to resign from the company, but they allowed me to be paid my bonus check for the first part of the year. I am clear the company did not give that money to me. God did. I was also sent additional checks that I truly did not expect to see or knew was coming. God again. I was able to go on un-employment and have plenty of money coming in so I could choose a perfect job for me, and take the time to work on myself, and my life from a spiritual perspective. I worked on the inside, and it manifested on the outside. I did everything that Terry suggested to do to obtain my goals and develop a prosperity consciousness.

So how do you make a goal, work to achieve it, while releasing the picture that it has to be exactly the way you visualize it, and not suffer until you have it?

GOAL SESSION

Making a goal is very important in trying to create what you want in your life. Just thinking about the goal or the outcome is not enough. Many experts such as Tony Robbins, Terry Cole-Whittaker, Deepak Chopra, and many others have written about the power of writing down our goals. All of these great authors have taken the same universal principles and laws and put it into a format that has worked for them. I have summarized their teachings and what has been helpful for me in achieving my goals and dreams.

First, visualize that on one end of the spectrum you have a goal, and on the other you have reality or where you sit currently. For example, if you have a goal to be a size 2, and currently you are a size 6, that is your spectrum. This is an example and a goal I had in my life. Where I have this example, replace your own goals and dreams to understand the process of achieving goals and manifesting your dreams. We all have the power to create our own lives and our own dreams. No two lives are the same, neither are the goals.

GOAL	CURRENT REALITY
Size 2	Size 6

There are steps that need to be taken to achieve your desired goal. Visualization is a very powerful technique that helps manifest dreams into reality, but visualization alone will not make your body transform. Tony Robbins gives the example that if you want to be successful, and just "bliss out", that is just sit in meditation and visualize and do not take action, someone is going to come and take your couch. Visualization and meditation are important steps in manifesting, because it gets you in touch with that creative being that is in each of us. Deepak Chopra refers to this as the law of pure potentiality. It allows us to become aware of the unlimited potential that we have, and what we are capable of creating.

When you visualize something you want in your life as if you already have it, your subconscious cannot tell the difference between something you imagine and something you actually experience. That is why it is important to only focus on positive experiences in life. This is why a repeated thought pattern of fear can manifest in your experience.

Whatever you focus on,
you'll move toward.

Back to our spectrum example, the desire to be a size 2, but where you stand today is a size 6. You have to ask these four important questions:

What are the steps that I need to take to achieve my goal?

Why do I want to achieve this goal?

What needs to be released?

What do I need to let go of that is no longer working for me?

The first question: *"What are the steps that I need to take to achieve my goal?"* These steps will turn into your action plan. For example,

GOAL   **CURRENT REALITY**

Size 2   Size 6

STEPS: Sign up for a gym

Work out 5-6 days per week

Get a personal trainer to learn weight routine

Eat 6 small meals per day

Drink 10, 8oz glasses of water per day

Taking the action is the most important part of the goal. You need to move toward the goal and get started. The steps are what it will take to succeed. Without the steps you have a goal that most likely will not be achieved. What will motivate you to take the steps? Your "Why"

The second question, *"Why do I want to achieve this goal?"* This "Why" will fuel your determination. If you get a big enough "Why" you will be driven to succeed. You need to have a "Why". Another way of thinking of your "Why" is, what feelings will achieving these goals give you? The feeling or the Why needs to be your focus. That is what will propel you in taking the steps to achieving your goals. Discipline sounds good, but it is not a driving force to move a person to action.

For example:

Why: I want to feel sexy.

I want to fit into my size 2 clothes.

I want to feel energetic and healthy.

I want to be proud of how I look.

I want to release my obsession/compulsions about how I look.

I want a new self-image.

Once you become really clear about what is going to keep you determined, and why you are motivated to move towards the goal, you need to ask the third question. *"What do I need to release?"* Think of the spectrum of where the goal is and where you are currently, as a road. Put in even more simple terms, point A to point B. What is in the road that will disguise itself as roadblocks? This could be other people, it could be your own limiting thoughts, it could be fears, or it could be your own beliefs. Maybe you have a belief that you couldn't possibly ever be a size 2, or maybe you feel you don't deserve to be. It is time to get really clear about what has stopped you in the past, and what has potential from stopping you now. If you become conscious of the roadblocks, and have clarity that they are there, you can release or avoid them.

Example:

Roadblocks: Eating junk food.

Eating too big of portions.

Eating too many bars.

Skipping workouts to sleep in.

Perfect Pictures.

Now that the goal has been set, you have committed to taking the actions, you have determined your motivation behind why you want to achieve the goal, and you have discovered anything that may keep you from the goal. Now it is time to see where you have perfect pictures.

You may reach for the heavens and only touch a star. The fact that you stretched yourself, you won. You improved yourself and you made the effort. The large majorities of people don't even look up, let alone reach out. The large majority of the population doesn't even make goals. Many are too afraid to dream, or too lazy to make it happen.

If for example, you wanted a new job making $75,000 per year (your goal) and make $50,000 (current reality), and you went for your goal. You took the steps you needed to take and you found a new job making $60,000. The person with perfect pictures would not be happy because he or she was attached to the goal of $75,000, even though you just improved your salary by $10,000 per year. It is the attachments and the lack of gratitude that will keep a person stuck in the box of "the way they think it needs to be". God may have a better plan. God may have surprises in store with this new job.

For my goal of having my ideal body, I forgot to be grateful. I was so determined to get to my size 4, and when I did, I still was not perfect. I then thought if I become a size 2, then I'll be perfect. I reached that goal, and it still was not good enough. I suffered the whole way instead of being so grateful for my new body.

I had gone from a size 10 to a size 2 and was still not happy. When you are grateful, you are in the present moment. You are happy with what is, but know that you can continue to achieve more if that is what you desire.

For example:

What I am grateful for: I have a strong, healthy body.

My body is improving everyday.

I have found a program that my body likes.

I have more energy.

There needs to be a balance between driving to achieve your ultimate dreams and desires, and for being happy with what is. It's a feeling of wanting something so badly, yet being detached with the outcome. It is a tough practice, but it can be done. When you find this balance, you can achieve your greatest dreams, yet enjoy your life as it is in the moment. Remember, happiness can only be found in the moment, and gratitude is a link to happiness.

GOAL   **CURRENT REALITY**

_____   _____

STEPS: _____

_____

_____

_____

Why: _____

_____

_____

_____

_____

Roadblocks: _____

_____

_____

_____

_____

What I am grateful for: _____

_____

_____

Determine what success means to you in your life. We all have a different way of defining success for ourselves. Do you define success by what possessions you have attained, or by your own personal achievements? What steps can you take today that will make you feel more successful? If you did your absolute best today what would it look like?

My personal definition of success: _____

_____

_____

_____

Determine what your purpose in life is. Imagine yourself at the end of your life. What would you have liked to have, done, or become in your lifetime? What is the one thing that you want to achieve in your lifetime that will enrich you and the lives of others?

My purpose is: _____

_____

_____

_____

Make sure to write down all of your desires and goals. Write out what you want to achieve or accomplish in your lifetime. As you start to dream and imagine your goals manifesting in your life, they will. Also write out the actions that you need to take immediately. Tony Robbins has a practice, "Never leave the site of a goal without doing something towards its achievement." Also make sure to read your goals when you awaken in the morning, and before you go to bed each night.

> ***"A goal that is not written down is merely a wish."***
> **Alexander Lockhart.**

Goals: **Immediate Actions:**

_____   _____

_____   _____

_____   _____

Terry Cole-Whittaker, Deepak Chopra, and Alexander Lockhart encourage people to get in touch with our special abilities and talents. Deepak Chopra wrote in The Seven Spiritual Laws of Success, "You have a unique talent and a unique way of expressing it. There is something that you can do better than anyone else in the whole world - and for every unique talent and unique expression of that talent, there are also unique needs. When these needs are matched with the creative expression of your talent that is the spark that creates affluence. Expressing your talents to fulfill needs creates unlimited wealth and abundance."

Write down all of your special talents and abilities. Concentrate on all the things you can do, and give praise to yourself for those abilities and talents. No one else in the universe is like you. Truly learn to embody that you are unique and special. We all have heard that at sometime in our lives and it can sound trite. When we embody that we are so unique, our lives have greater meaning. We are an individualized expression of God and were given the talents and abilities to use in God's service.

My special talents: _____

_____

_____

_____

_____

"It has been said that 40% of the things we worry about never happen; 30% of the things we worry about we can't change; 12% of our worries are about health; 10% of our time spent worrying is on petty and miscellaneous things; and 8% of our worry time is on real problems. Therefore 92% of the things we worry about can be avoided"

Alexander Lockhart

What do you worry about on a consistent basis? When you are worrying you are creating negative circumstances in your life. You are keeping joy and abundance at bay. When you focus on positive thoughts and what you want to create that will be your reality. Worry truly is a worthless emotion. When we worry, we do not have faith. When we worry we are in our ego, thinking that we can control outcomes that are out of our control. When we have faith we trust in a power much greater than ourselves to make everything happen in divine order. When we worry we are not in the present moment. In the present moment is where you can find joy and surrender.

My worry list: _____

_____

_____

Learn to love yourself exactly the way you are right here and right now. There are actions that you need to take to achieve the goals in your life. If you are dissatisfied in areas of your life, you can work to change those conditions. We don't want to stay focused on those parts of our lives that we wish we could change, because we want to focus on that which gives us a better self-esteem. We need to recognize just how great and special we really are. List all of your great qualities. Recognize how truly special and beautiful you are.

Things I like about myself: _____

_____

_____

_____

_____

To really take a quantum leap in your life as far as setting and achieving goals, contact The Anthony Robbins Company for the program Get The Edge. If you truly apply the teachings, wonderful changes will transpire in your life. It has in mine.

6.

Prosperity Consciousness

DOING THIS PRACTICE TAKES WORK. To change your thoughts you truly need to be a warrior. The big you, the real you, the higher mind, needs to pay attention to the thoughts in the ego mind. When I started to pay attention to my own thoughts, I was amazed at what I was telling myself. As the warrior, I needed to pay attention and then change the thoughts immediately.

Any negative, self-defeating thoughts that do not serve you need to be changed in order to have more light. All of the fear, lack, and limitation created by the mind can be changed. It takes work. Think of the sub-conscious mind as an old record playing the same thing over and over. In order to change the tune, the old record needs to be stopped. This takes paying attention, and saying, "stop", or "cancel" to the old thoughts. Then create new higher thoughts and replace the old with the new. One of the first ways that I started to change my thoughts was to pray, read, listen to tapes and, as often as possible, I attended classes on spirituality and church. I also read my mantras several times every day.

I had been reading books on spirituality and self-improvement for years. It is easy to get the concepts on an intellectual level, but to truly change one has to embody the concepts. The journey has to be of one of mind and heart in communion. For example, I had read The Four Agreements, By Don Miguel Ruiz a few years ago. I remember thinking that the teaching was amazing and made so much sense. It wasn't until I started attending the church that the minister would do his services based on these Four Agreements. He created a couple's retreat based on these agreements. He conducted a "Dreaming a New Dream" seminar based on the agreements. Finally, a "Creative Living" class that I attended was based on these Four Agreements. I did not just get it intellectually like I did years before, but I embodied the teachings. I now have four new agreements in my life. And it has transformed my life.

Prayer and Treatment:

The power of prayer is amazing. There are millions of stories on how prayer had healed the sick, or improved a person life.

Toni's Story

Toni is a woman that had been married to her husband for many years. One morning she awoke and found she had fallen out of love with her husband. She communicated this to her husband,

and was hoping for a divorce. Her husband begged her to give him another chance. Every night while she was sleeping he held his hand over her body and prayed that Toni would be able to open her heart to him again. Toni's husband prayed for months, and finally one day Toni found herself back in love with her husband.

I have experienced the power of prayer in my own life many times. I tried for years to quit smoking, only to find myself failing every time. I finally looked to God as my strength to help me quit. I prayed every night that I had the strength to become a non-smoker. I would visualize myself as living a life as a non-smoker, and then I would pray. One day a situation happened where a friend of mine told me that his wife was pregnant. She still continued to smoke despite the fact that she was pregnant, and was aware of the consequences. She had a child from a previous marriage and smoked all throughout her pregnancy. This child developed respiratory problems. Here she was pregnant with his child, and there was nothing he could do about it. I always told myself that there were two things that would get me to stop smoking. First, when I had become a career woman, wearing all of my different colored suits, I would quit. The other was when I became pregnant. Well, here I was wearing one of my business suits, involved in a successful career, and I still smoked. I did not foresee myself getting pregnant any time soon, as I was not involved with anyone at the time. But I thought to myself, "What makes me think that I will be able to quit smoking when I get pregnant, when I can't stop right now?" That night I smoked my last cigarette. To this day, whenever I have the desire or the habit thought to smoke, I turn to God, and he takes the desire away from me. I rarely have the desire or a thought to smoke a cigarette anymore, because I have changed my habit and my identity. Where at one point, it was so hard to go without smoking, I now can't imagine ever doing it again. Similar to releasing my perfect pictures, in the beginning it took vigilance, but with work and prayer, it is now second nature.

The funny thing about prayer is that prayer works for the person that actually says the prayer. It is us that respond to our prayers the minute they are said.

Treatment:

A new type of prayer that I was introduced to was treatment, or mind treatment. This is a spiritual practice that is practiced at the church. I was fully introduced into this practice and how to do it myself when I attended the class "Creative Living". It is very simple, yet very powerful. The power of treatment has helped me change my anger, my weight issues, and my perfect pictures, which brought more happiness and peace to my life.

The five steps to a treatment are:

1. God is . . .
2. I am . . .
3. I accept or I refuse
4. I give thanks
5. And so it is . . .

I am a visual person, so it helped for me to learn this practice by visualizing my hand. Similar to how we drew hand turkeys when we were kids. The thumb is the "God is" part. This part is where you declare all that God is.

For example:

God is love, light, and life.

The pointer finger is "I am". This is where you declare that you are one with God.

I am one with this love, this light, with life. I am an individualized expression of God.

The middle finger is "I accept" or "I refuse". This is where you give up or embody all that you need to be more at peace, or experience whatever you are treating for. This is also where you accept that you have the power, and you claim it to the universe.

I no longer accept the agreement that I need to be perfect. I accept that I can create the life that I want and the form I want my body to take. I now, in this moment, refuse to have any type of self-hatred, self-dislike, or self-disapproval, for it does not serve me. I accept for myself unconditional love and self-approval. I know that I am already a perfect spiritual being.

The ring finger is "I give thanks".

I look up and give thanks for all of the wonderful things in my life. I give thanks for my spirituality and my willingness to change. I give thanks for the knowing that I have the power to change.

The pinky finger is the "And so it is". This is where you release the treatment to the Universe.

I know this to be my new agreement, and I know it is so, And so it is!

This practice has been so powerful. Any time I feel fear, anger, resentment, jealousy, competition, or anything that I know will keep me from my peace, I do a treatment. A treatment can be about love, prosperity, wealth, happiness, forgiveness, impeccability, freedom, or anything that will help the mind be free from negativity.

Treatment is not to be used to try to change someone else or someone else's mind. It is for the person doing the treatment.

Reading:

I try to make it a practice that I read some type of spiritual book each night. Even if it is only a few pages, the written words can help a mind shift from negative to higher thoughts. When I was off of work, I read 7 different books, and I learned pearls from each of those books. I highlighted the most important parts of the books and I typed them up for myself. I bounded the books and read something everyday to help remind me of the words that once moved me. This has helped me embody the teachings of the books.

The book The Four Agreements by Don Miguel Ruiz was a large part of my transformation. To truly embody the four agreements, helped change my life. I can't stress enough what a difference it can make in a person's life to embody the works of these teachings instead of just merely reading the words. By making four new agreements with myself, my life has become so wonderful. All four of the agreements shifted the way I live in the world. If I attended Terry Cole-Whittaker's seminar and listened to her teachings, that would be informative, however to truly experience significant change in my life, I would need to make the teachings apart of my own life. Similar to reading and listening to everything there is to know about God, you would not have the direct experience until you developed the relationship with him yourself. This meant actually doing treatments, saying affirmations, reading books, and meditating. Reading books and listening to spiritual tapes and spiritual music is putting higher thoughts into the mind and into the cells of the body.

When you think about cells and that cells are be re-generated every minute in a person's body, what type of energy do you want those cells born into? I think of a song from the artist Pink. She is a great singer and her music has a great beat, but one of her songs I have to turn off every time I hear it. The lyrics are not ones that I want to have running through my head for my sub-conscious to take hold of. Some of the lyrics are "don't let me get me, I'm my own worst enemy". Why would I want that in my head? I don't. There is also a song on the radio, by Nos. The lyrics are, "I know I can, be what I want to be. If I work hard at it, I'll be where I want to be". I do want these thoughts running through my head. I have been listening to music that is fun, but also has lyrics about abundance and being one with spirit. I have stopped and listened to my mind and have caught myself many times repeating over and over the lyrics in the spiritual songs. Those are phrases I want running through my mind. These songs will only bring more happiness and joy into my life.

Mantras/Affirmations:

I laughed when I first heard the notion of repeating mantras over and over. It reminded me of the skit on Saturday Night Live. Stewart Smaley would sit in front of a mirror and say:

I'm Good Enough
I'm Smart Enough
And Dog Gone it, People like me.

As funny as it may sound, it works! Repeating affirmations has amazing power in the sub-conscious mind. An affirmation is a positive, goal-oriented statement spoken with conviction to yourself in the first person. Alexander Lockhart wrote in <u>Positive Charges</u>, "Affirmations are based on the way you would like things to be. They are stated as if the goal or desire has already been achieved. The use of positive affirmations means developing a habit of replacing negative messages with positive reinforcements. As these positive messages become part of your subconscious, they will soon be brought into your reality." Alexander gives great guidelines for using affirmations to have them be effective:

1. They must be personal. For example, use the "I am", "I do", and "I will" statements.

2. They must be positive. Affirmations must be positive statements and should affirm what you are moving toward, not away from.

3. They must be in the present tense. Don't use words like "someday" or "soon".

4. They must be specific. For example, instead of saying, "I will make a lot of money" say, "I make _____ amount of dollars per year."

5. They must be believable. You must believe in yourself and your abilities. Don't set your aim so high that you can't imagine or accept what you want to accomplish.

Create your own mantra or affirmation that is personal to you. Use the guidelines that Alexander Lockhart explained to make your own dreams a reality. Be open to the experience and see how the affirmations work in your life. When we are open to new experiences and do what other successful people have done that have gone before us, we will experience the same results. Many of the successful leaders work with affirmations such as Terry Cole-Whittaker, Tony Robbins, Dr. Wayne Dyer, Marianne Williamson, and Deepak Chopra.

I work with the mantra "God is My Source and Supply" on a daily basis. Just that one mantra has changed my life. I don't look for other people, places, or things to be my supply. I truly believe that my supply comes from the unlimited and infinite Spirit. I am now aware that no one organization is the source of my money. For if I was to loose my job, there would be another one available to me, because my supply comes from God. I learned that first hand. My supply of love does not come from my husband he is an avenue that God works through.

Some affirmations that I have worked into my daily life that have made a significant difference:

I, _____ do not take what other people say, do, feel, or think personally.

By not taking things personally, I _____ increase my personal power.

I am safe and secure in my world.

I deserve joy.

The willingness to realize that there are things in your life that are stopping you from having joy, peace, happiness, prosperity, or whatever you desire is the first step. Many people are too afraid to look at their lives. Many of us have fallen asleep to what is, and to awake or become conscious is very scary. Many people fear that if they look at what needs to be changed, they will not know how to change. They then realize that there is something "wrong" with them. The truth is each one of us has the power. It takes work if a person truly wants transformation. This journey of transformation is why we are all here. As much work as you put into yourself, is as much growth that you will experience in your life. What you sow you will reap. We invest so much time and energy in our families, friends, and careers. What about ourselves? What about our spirituality?

Spirituality is not just about going to church on Sundays. Spirituality is having the knowing that you are apart of something so much bigger than our own little worlds. We are all here for a higher purpose. When we put limitations on ourselves, or have too high of expectations, we are not able to do our life's work. When you release that which binds you, you are finally free. You are then a direct channel that God can work through. Being connected is allowing God to work through you in every aspect of your life.

Spirituality is not something just reserved while you are at church. We are all spirits having a human experience. The spirit connection can be brought into every aspect of family, friends, careers, and ourselves.

Change can be extremely scary. Change is the one thing in life, besides God, that is consistent. The only constant is God and the spiritual world. When I realized that Spirit is constant, and that I am an individualized expression of Spirit, I then knew that I could create what I wanted regardless of whatever is happening in my life. There is nothing else in the physical world that is constant. People change, money devaluates, companies fail, the world is designed for change.

Deepak Chopra wrote about the 7 Spiritual Laws of Success. One of the laws is Detachment. This is the wisdom of uncertainty. In the willingness to accept uncertainty, the more freedom we will experience. To be attached to an idea, or a picture, we are attached to our past, from the known, which he referred to as the prison of past conditioning. When we surrender ourselves into God, Spirit, the Universe, we allow the creative mind to work. We then will have faith, trust, and accept that everything is unfolding in our lives for our greatest and best.

One of our needs as humans is to have uncertainty, or surprise. In the past I used to obsess over something until it manifested. For example, if I was waiting to hear the news if I was going to receive a job offer, I would constantly think about when I would receive the offer, and become very impatient. I would then worry what the offer was going to be, how the interview went, and if I was actually going to get the job. My mind would go to worry and obsession. Now I practice wonderment. I anticipate that what I want will happen, and there is excitement in not knowing exactly when it will manifest. I do my best, practice detachment, and trust that everything will work out perfectly. It always does.

Bringing God In

Marianne Williamson, best-selling author and lecturer on the Course in Miracles, shares her experience of when she first brought God into her life. She thought that God was just going to add to what she already had. As she put it he was going to come in and spruce things up a bit. She thought of her life as a house and God was going to come in and put a portico in the front, maybe put up some curtains. Instead when she invited God into her life it was as if a wrecking ball came and flattened the whole house down to the base. In that she was able to start fresh, and God said, "Can we begin now?"

I had the same type of experience. When I invited Spirit in and started to meditate, my life flipped upside down. Earlier I shared what I went through when I lived in Chicago. I had my life all together on the outside, but on the inside felt very empty and disconnected. I went from a high paying job, my little size 4 body, money in the bank investments, many great friends that surrounded me, I was a non-smoker, and I had a boyfriend.

I moved to California. I found mediation and the deep connection I was looking for. Within a few months I was unemployed, a size 10, $60,000 in debt, I broke up with my boyfriend, and I did not have any friends living near me. God came in with the wrecking ball and then started all over. During the time that I was going through this transformation, it was challenging. I had nothing to cling to in the physical world, but I was very connected spiritually. I felt like my life up until this point was like being Jane of the jungle. I would always end up swinging from vine to vine. My next move was always effortlessly in front of me. All of a sudden there was no vine in front of me to grab onto. I had to go within. I had to learn how to trust Spirit. Now, exactly five years later, I am the happiest I have ever been. I am a size 4. I have a great marriage to a wonderful man. I have a stepson who gives me so much love. I have a connection to Spirit that is unwavering. I have a spiritual community at the Redding Church of Religious Science. I have a new job with a great pharmaceutical company where I can truly be myself. I am out of debt and investing wisely. My husband and I are building our dream home. I have a great number of friends and sources of love.

I have an abundance of love, happiness, and joy in my life. I have found my passion.

Meditation:

Meditation for me has been one of the greatest ways that I connect to spirit. For me, meditation is a clear and deliberate act of consistently, relentlessly, and joyfully putting myself in the path of Spirit. Even if 99.99 percent of my meditation is mind chatter, the difference in my life has been profound. When I take the time to sit and slow down, I am making the effort to connect to the Divine presence. Meditation grounds and centers me and brings me back to my heart and present moment.

There are days that meditating comes very easy, and other days that it is a great effort to keep my mind focused. There are countless ways to meditate. There are different techniques that are taught many different ways. Just having the intention to connect with spirit, practicing meditation, no matter what type, will be the avenue to get you there. I mentioned earlier that "Awakening Your Light Body" was a very intense form of meditation. These are tapes that are guided meditations and can be used to transform a person's life. The tapes help individuals take a quantum leap in their development and growth. Some of the meditation tapes include sub-personality journey, getting in touch with your power, happiness, manifesting, abundance, etc. The tapes work with different energy centers in the body such as the emotional body, the heart center, the head center, and the light body. These tapes have made a profound difference in my life. As with most meditation practices, working with energy is what creates the intense changes.

In many of the tapes you are asked to find yourself in a beautiful meadow. You use visualization to imagine yourself in whatever a meadow is to you, using your "pictures". You then meet a part of yourself called a sub-personality. It wants to be transformed or brought to a higher light. Instead of throwing anger or negative energy at this sub-personality, you love this part of yourself. This is a different concept than most of us are familiar with. If we are aware beings and there are parts of ourselves that we do not like about ourselves, we usually shame or hate that part of ourselves. This is a different approach to where you love that part of you. You show and have compassion for that part, because it is doing the best job it knows how, to help you in some area of your life. It has just been taught to do it in a way that does not serve anymore, and it just needs the love and guidance of how to evolve. This all sounded very strange to me when I first heard the concept. I was so desperate to change that I was very open. The changes that have manifested in my life because of these tapes have been amazing.

Other types of meditation that I do to help embody my new concepts about myself, or my mantras, is to sit up right with my legs crossed. There are energy centers throughout the body, called chakras. There are seven chakras, or energy centers in a person's body.

When the first chakra, which is at the base of the spine, is balanced and open, you feel abundant, in good health, and connected to your body. This center is associated with the color of red.

When the second chakra is aligned, you feel connected to other people and yourself. This chakra is located below your belly button between the hipbones and is associated with the color of orange.

The third chakra is the center for personal power and emotional control. This center is located directly beneath the rib cage, where the two ribs come together. This center is associated with the color of yellow.

The fourth chakra is your heart center, and when it is open you feel safe, able to trust, able to take risks, love yourself, and also feel loved. This center is associated with the color of green.

The fifth chakra, which is associated with the color of dark blue, is your throat center. When this center is open it allows you to communicate with truth and clarity, express yourself clearly, and speak your true feelings with love.

The sixth chakra, also known as the "third eye", opens your psychic and intuitive abilities. This center is associated with the color of purple, and is located between the eyes, just slightly above the eyebrows.

Finally, the crown center, or the seventh chakra, located at the top of your head, is your spiritual center and is your connection to your Higher Self, imagination, and awareness of other dimensions. This center is associated with the color of red and can be visualized like a spinning disk.

Many people are not even aware of what a chakra is, but feel that certain situations or people control their emotions, feelings, or power. When these centers are awakened, aligned, and cleared from other people there is a deeper connection to spirit and oneself.

I take my mantras, for example, God is my Source and Supply, and contemplate the mantra and run the centers while placing that mantra in the center. As I visualize the chakra, I spin the energy for the old beliefs and energy to be released while putting in the new belief, the new mantra. I do that for each of the energy centers.

There are so many different types of meditations and many are available in books and tapes if you are a beginner. To start just sit quietly and think about God. Make yourself open to communicate with Spirit. That silent time alone, getting in touch with Spirit, will make a difference. Get in touch with the God or Goddess within yourself. Know the truth of who you are. The process of self-realization is amazing and deep. Personal and spiritual growth is like peeling an onion. To get to the core, there are many layers that need to be peeled off. The rewards are tremendous. One has to be willing to look at the parts that are not working in life. The first step in AA, or any of the 12 step programs, is first admitting that there is a problem. Many people are in denial of their lives, or have fallen asleep. The next step is to be willing to make the changes, and having the knowing that you are powerful to change. Next is to make the decision to change.

Finally, and most importantly, do the work. My life is wonderful. I am very blessed. What I had to go through was completely worth where I am in life now. I needed to release thoughts and energy in my body that did not serve me. In order to get from where I was and to get to where I wanted to go, there were things in my way that needed to be removed. The lessons in life and experiences along the way are those things that needed to be removed. The easiest way to remove something is to replace it with something else. Instead of giving up cigarettes, I needed to adopt myself as a non-smoker. In order to give up needing approval from other people, I needed to embody the agreement that

I don't take anything personally. In order to give up fear, I needed to embody courage.

Where in your life do you need to make changes?

Have you made the decision to change?

What are your reasons for making the decision to change?

How do you feel deep down inside?

How do you really feel about yourself and your life?

Are you willing to do the work, the practice in order to have profound changes in your life?

What are the pros and cons of continuing in the direction you are going?

Do you want to create a brighter future?
Then do it. Be, then Do, and you will Have.

7.

Asking the Important Questions

ONCE I REALIZED THAT I had "perfect pictures", I had to dig deeper and find out why I had them. What purpose were they serving? Where did my perfect pictures come from? Why do I have them? For me, it boiled down to wanting approval from others. I was always so concerned how things would look to other people, and how they would approve or disapprove of me. Every time I would take a trip home to visit my family, I felt like I needed to loose weight. My family is very attentive to outer appearances and I always wanted to look good to gain their approval. When I was a size 2, I received a great deal of approval, especially from my mom. I would get more attention; I got the approval I was looking for. When I came home and I was a size 10, there was a great deal of disapproval. I needed to fix my weight and change it by going on a diet. Here I was the most spiritually connected than I have ever been, but also the heaviest, and I was truly not seen. When I lost all my weight, and I was size 2 again, I would get condemnation in a different way. "Don't loose anymore weight". My family thought I was becoming too thin. I felt like it was never good enough. This was all my perspective, and because I always felt disapproval, I would get very angry. I was unclear about who I was, and so I looked to other people to define me. What I learned was a very important realization that changed my life. I took everything so personally. I looked to other people's opinions of me instead of standing in the truth of who I was. I was able to release the agreement that what other people say, do, think, or feel was because of me. I then adopted the agreement that I would not take things personally, and by not taking things personally, I increased my personal power. This one agreement alone changed my life.

Russ

My husband and I have a friend who used to push my buttons like nobody's business. I thought my mom pushed my buttons, but that was nothing compared to Russ. Russ, just being Russ, would say things, and I would find myself enraged. For example, one night he and his wife were over for dinner. I received a phone call from a woman that I taught with at the Church. We teach the children's church as part of tithing. We were playing phone tag via our message machines. I do not like to answer the phone when I have guest over, so I let the machine pick up the call. The machine was in the kitchen, as were we. The woman started leaving a message and mentioned Sunday's curriculum. She said we will do the "God candle", which is where you light the candle and the kids say what God means to them. She said, "God is Love", and Russ made a horrible face and made fun of her and said, "God is love" in a very sarcastic voice. His wife told him that what he said was very rude. I agreed with her, and found myself very upset. I went into the bathroom to figure out why I was so upset. I didn't realize at the time, but I took what he said very personally. I also needed his approval. I thought he was going to think I wasn't cool.

I shared this experience in the "Creative Living" class and the minister asked me, why do you care what he thinks? I couldn't answer him. I so much wanted Russ's approval, but I did not know why. This caused me great suffering.

Other similar situations happened where Russ had said something that was very hurtful to me. I took it very personally, and then would get angry instead of hurt. It would really bother me because he and his wife are our closet friends. They are great people. I hated feeling these feelings, and my husband hated when I was acting in this way. It put a strain on our relationship. The teachers in our lives are those who challenge us, and who push our buttons. They provide us an opportunity to receive value and transcend our experiences. Our response to these types of people is often to become angry with them to try to create some type of guilt for them. My behavior on many occasions was very inappropriate and we almost lost them as friends. During a separation from their friendship I adopted an agreement: I don't take anything personally.

I also adopted the agreement to stand in the truth of who I am. I now recognize that other people have their own opinions in which they are entitled to have. I used to need the approval of everyone and because of that need I would not stand in my own truth. I have also learned that approval seeking is something we learned to do at a very young age. Approval seeking is looking for our own value in the opinion of others. When we accept other people's opinions of ourselves we are saying that their opinion is more important than the opinions that we have of ourselves. When you become upset, immobilized, depressed, out of sorts, or unhappy with the way that someone else has treated you or behaved towards you because of what someone else has said or done, what you are really saying in that moment is "What that person thinks of me is more important than what I think of myself". Instead of standing in our own truth of who we are, we allow other people to define us. We are swayed by their picture of who we should be, instead of being unconditionally accepted for who we are. We need to get to a place where we recognize that someone else has an opinion, and they are entitled to their opinion. They are even entitled to their opinion of me. However, it doesn't say who I am and it doesn't validate who I am. Who I am is how I choose to process my life. I know the truth of me.

As a society, we have been raised with approval seeking. We were raised to go to school and to try to please our teachers. Our parents taught us that getting their approval was more important than anything else. We were to do what we were told to do. If we did not receive the approval we were seeking as a child as an adult we continue to try to attain that approval. We need to understand that searching for other people's approval of ourselves is not what is going to make us happy. Wanting, enjoying and even loving approval from others feels great. Having acceptance from the people that we care about makes us feel good. Dr. Wayne Dyer discussed in <u>Erroneous Zones</u> that where we get into trouble is having the need for approval. Need is something that you can't survive without such as oxygen, sleep, and food. If you need approval that means that you become immobilized without it. You have your self-esteem located in the wrong place. Self-esteem means self. It is located in the self, not in others.

I have since been able to cultivate a great relationship with not only Russ, but my mom as well. I don't let other people's opinions of me affect me the way it used to. I know the truth of who I am. I stand in my truth. I am an individualized expression of Spirit, perfect and complete. I visualize individual people in their own minds. Each person lives in his or her own dream. They have their own set of beliefs, opinions, pictures, judgments, feelings, ideas, and experiences.

I also realize and recognize that God is my source and that no one else is the cause of anything in my life, good or bad. No one is the cause of my happiness or despair. No one is the reason that I feel loved or rejected. With God as my source, I am the cause and the source in my own life. I decided not to give other people my power any more.

Other people do not judge the way we judge, or think the way we think. Russ ended up being one of my greatest spiritual teachers. This is an area where I realized that I took other people's opinions of myself over my own and it was a problem in my life. How was I to change this? I had to be a warrior on this and every issue. I would go as far as determining how I felt about myself based on if I received compliments from others; specifically, my husband. If I would get dressed up, or even stand naked in front of him, and did not receive a compliment, I would feel badly about myself. I would start the perfect pictures and start looking for areas of my body that needed to be changed in order for me to be perfect, for him to be wowed every time he looked at me.

Because I did not receive a compliment, I would think that he did not find me attractive anymore. This was such a self-defeating behavior and was unrealistic expectations put on my husband.

Mount Shasta

We went on a trip to Mount Shasta, a romantic weekend just the two of us. I looked great, but in my mind I did not think I did. I put on a bathing suit, and usually when I put on a suit he would make a compliment or whistle. I was walking around the cabin for a while and he was not even looking at me. I immediately started the "perfect" drama in my head. If he didn't compliment or acknowledge my body it must have been because of me (taking things personally and also making assumptions). I started in the mirror with "my thigh, my butt ..." It was not personal. He had some stuff on his mind and did not even realize that I put a bathing suit on. He was planning the day for us and was distracted. Instead of me knowing how great I looked, I looked to him to tell me how I should feel about myself. I looked in the mirror and instead of noticing all the beautiful things about my body and feeling confident, I trashed myself. Now I look in the mirror and notice the beauty. I appreciate and accept how I look. I do have the power to create whatever form I want to. If I do desire to be lean, I can take the steps to create the body I want by working out, eating less, and watching what I eat. That is my choice, my option. I will not look through my "perfect" lenses and be negative about myself. I wont even take myself personally.

When I now walk out of the bathroom, I have already filled myself up, and I am confident. I feel great about me. If Mike does compliment me, I let it further deepen the feelings I have about myself. I don't have any expectations that he needs to compliment me. I don't look to be filled by him, because I am already filled up. If he does not happen to compliment me, I don't take it personally, because I know the truth about me. I don't rely on his compliments to determine how I am going to feel about myself. This has not only brought so much aliveness and happiness into my existence, but our relationship is so much healthier.

Other people's opinions are just that. When you are connected to spirit and stand in your truth, and truly love yourself, other people's opinions and acceptance is not important.

Cheerleaders

Because of the great power and feelings of tithing, I donate some of my time on Sundays to teach the children's church. I also was guided to become a cheerleading coach at one of the local junior high schools. This was such a great experience for me and was a true gift from Spirit. The girls thought that I was their cheer advisor, but it turns out that I became their spiritual advisor. These girls were so wonderful, but a lot of them were very unclear of who they are. At that age they are so concerned with appearances, and they are so sensitive. They take things very personally. I knew that being their cheer advisor was a way for me to work for God, by working with these girls. My job was to empower them, and to help them realize the greatness that is within each and every one of them.

One of the girls was having a bad day and felt everyone was mad at her. I even had to get firm with her, because she was not practicing with the rest of the squad. I could tell she was just crushed. I took her outside to discuss not taking things so personally. In her mind everything was about her, when in reality other people do things because of themselves not because of her. She got it and has on many occasions respectfully said to myself, and to others, "That is your opinion". I feel such power coming from her that she is not being crushed by another person's words. She is learning who she is. At that age they think the whole world revolves around them. When they are given the consciousness that what other people do, say, think or feel is not because of them, they feel empowered. As a retired Pom girl, I know the pressure that is put on being the "leaders" of the school. There is also a lot of negative energy that the girls get thrown at them by jealous and envious girls. The whole squad and I had the conversation about them not really being who they think they are. They are not their roles as cheerleaders. They are not their bodies. They are not their grades. They are not their boyfriends. They are not their parents or friends. They are not their emotions. They are a spirit soul, and that is the truth of them. They are so beyond what people perceive of them, and they are so much more than they know of themselves. The girls feel empowered, because they are learning the truth of who they are.

I ask them to ask themselves ... "Why is the affecting me? What is the cause of my suffering?" I continued to ask myself what other issues were there besides desiring the approval of others? My "perfect pictures" were also because I was very attached to the way I thought it should be. It needed to be my way.

The Kit Kat

I was at the gym one morning, feeling good about my new way of thinking about my body, and releasing my perfect pictures. There are lessons in every moment, and I was presented with yet another one. I had started to loose weight and feel so much better about myself, and my body. I made a new agreement that I could create whatever I wanted to, yet be detached from perfection. This approach to loving myself automatically resulted in me eating healthier. I was eating in ways that helped me create the body I wanted. All of a sudden, I am on the treadmill and a man goes around the cardio room and starts handing everyone king size Kit Kats. I immediately went into the "Oh, No!" I had perfect pictures about food. Because I had my pictures about my weight, I also was obsessive and compulsive about food. I had a major issue with food. I had a picture that there are "bad" foods and "good" foods. I remember my mom always saying, "Oh, I was so bad this weekend", or "I've been so good" and she was referring to what she had eaten. I adopted that. How sad that I told myself I was either good or bad based on what I ate. What a horrible way to relate to yourself and to food. Food is not either good or bad, it is just food. Some foods are healthier than others and create either abundance, or a deficiency of energy for the body. This realization came to me the minute the gentleman gave me the Kit Kat.

I had been focusing on my beautiful parts of my body and loving my body. Because I desired to create more beauty, I focused on that. By focusing on the things you love, your subconscious will believe that you look beautiful. If you tell yourself you are fat, your subconscious will hear that and will continue to create what you think. I was focusing on my mantras:

I, _____, am a complete, perfect being just the way I am.

91

I, _____, choose to eat to sustain and nourish my physical body.

I, _____, have no need to use food to fill me up because I love myself just as I am.

When you truly love yourself, it takes the energy off of the food. I was reading my mantras on the treadmill and a Kit Kat gets delivered to me. He gave everyone in the room a free fundraiser candy bar. He helped out a local school by purchasing the candy, and then he gave them away. He felt good and also made others feel good. I showed appreciation, but at the same time, I panicked. "This Kit Kat was bad. I have to get rid of it. I'll give it to Mike, no Ryan, no I'll throw it away so it is not in the house to tempt me". Those were my thoughts. Just then I realized that just a couple of nights ago at a friends dinner party Mike had given me a few bites of a blondie brownie. I truly tasted how wonderful it was. It was a little piece, but enough to truly taste how delicious and sweet it was. I felt satisfied. I didn't feel the need to go and get my own piece. There was no energy on the brownie "good" or "bad", "right" or "wrong". It was just a yummy dessert. I ate it, I enjoyed it, and that was it. No guilt, shame, judgment, or self-hatred was put on myself. It occurred to me that the "perfect picture" to me was that to obtain my ideal body, I needed to "eat perfect" and the Kit Kat would prevent me from doing that. That would be bad. I thought why can't I just see it as what it is, a candy bar, very sweet and very good. Take the "perfect" energy off of it and it doesn't have any power over me.

I do not need this Kit Kat to fill me up, because I am already filled up with God's love.

In that moment, I broke the obsession and the need to be perfect, and the energy was taken off of the candy bar. I know one of my sub-personalities is a rebel. She does not like anyone or anything telling her what to do. When one part of myself tells her you can't have that, all she wants is what is being denied. She usually takes over the mind and ends up getting what she wants anyways. Many "dieters" know this well. Many people tell themselves they are going to be good, and follow a certain plan. A cookie somehow ends up in front of them. The cookie is then digested in their stomach, and they didn't even remember tasting it! That was a very familiar scenario for me. I learned this when I stopped smoking, but until that day I was delivered the Kit Kat did not realize that it also applies to food, more so sweets. When I quit smoking, because it was not serving me, I had to dialogue with parts of my personality. Whenever I had the desire come up to have a cigarette I would say, "Hey, the choice is yours. You can have a cigarette, but realize that if you smoke you probably will be hooked again. The choice is yours. Do you want to be back into that addiction and habit again, or do you want to remain a non-smoker, healthy, clean, and beautiful?" She has always picked the later. The point is that the energy is completely off of "No, you can't" or talking badly to her or threatening her. If I did that in the areas of smoking, I would be back where I didn't want to be. The same is true for the unhealthy way I obsessively ate sweets. We always have choices. Now I tell myself that I choose to eat a certain way or have certain foods instead of saying that I can't. For example, my husband and I have been not eating complex carbohydrates after 4pm. If I think to eat something that has carbohydrates, I tell myself that I can have it tomorrow before 4pm. I never tell myself I can't have it. I choose not to have it because I know my body will be leaner if I wait.

We are free to choose in every area of our lives. There will be consequences in each of the choices that we make. Do you choose heaven or hell; fear or love; freedom or enslavement? Many people are so miserable in their lives just based on what they create with their minds. They are living out of fear, afraid to live. As souls, we did not take a body, and God did not give us life to be in hell. Hell is not some place where everything is hot and you have an evil man with a pitchfork that will laugh meanly at you. Hell is a place that many people are creating while they are alive.

It is a consciousness in our own minds. It is a state of being and a mindset. You can create Heaven or Hell. The choice is yours. God wants us to have all that we desire, spiritually and materially. It is said in the bible, "It is God's pleasure to give you the kingdom".

My Doctor Friend

I have a customer that I call on, who is also a friend. We have had many discussions on what his perfect mate looks like, acts like, etc. He himself has "perfect pictures" and has admitted that once he finds out a woman has imperfections, he looses interest. He then finds himself with wandering eyes, because if the person he is with is not the "perfect one", someone else out there must be. He said that he is never truly satisfied with what is in his life, because he knows the way he wants it, and he is attached to the way it should be (in his mind).

By looking at his perfect picture that he knew was unrealistic, he was able to figure out where this picture came from. For years he was telling himself a lie. He told himself that his three marriages failed because he is incapable of having a long-term relationship. He was absolutely amazing at accomplishing anything he sought out to do, but in the area of relationships, he felt he was a complete failure.

When he took a much deeper look at his life, he realized that these perfect pictures were there as a survival tool that he used when he was a child. When he was a small child his mother had a great deal of emotional problems, and was also an alcoholic. His mother always had some type of drama going on around her. In order for him to survive as a small child, he developed a defense mechanism. He would run as far away from her as he could so that he would not have to see her in one of her episodes. He went off and took care of himself and got his mind on other things that gave him joy, like playing with his friends. This sub-personality was initially developed to keep him from pain. Many years later this sub-personality was no longer serving him and needed to be evolved, because it was causing him pain.

After his third divorce, and accepting the fact that long-term relationships always ended in failure for him, he took a much deeper look. He realized that at any point in any of his relationships when the women had any emotional issues or drama, he felt the need to run. In the beginning of relationships everyone is on their best behavior, but eventually each person has stuff that comes out. Once he saw that the women were not perfect and they possessed drama, he became uninterested and turned off. He would run away from the relationship and the woman, similar to how he ran as a small child. As a child, he ran to survive emotionally. All these years he kept the agreement that in order to survive, he needed to run away when women were having drama in their lives. As an adult, this agreement no longer served him. He realized he had perfect pictures. He then realized why he had the perfect pictures. His next step was to release the agreement that led him to feel that everything needed to be perfect. He knew that if he was to ever love again, his current expectations of a "perfect" woman were not realistic, and it was keeping him suffering in his life. The truth is that everything is perfect. The universe is not set up as a haphazard event. There are no coincidences. It is a perfect enfoldment of life. Once we understand that, we are not left to suffer. He was once stuck in his pictures, and use to feel that he did not need to change to find happiness. He wanted it the way he wanted it, and felt it would happen. He would one day find the perfect woman that did not have any emotional issues. He just may, but the suffering in his search, was that worth it? He did not feel it was, and was willing to release what was no longer working in his life.

Rebecca's Pictures

Rebecca is one of my greatest spiritual teachers and soul sister on this life journey. She came to me as my therapist, and turned out to be a very dear friend. Rebecca is a Light Body worker and a spiritual warrior. She has been on a spiritual quest for years. One day she found herself married with two great kids, and very connected to Spirit. She realized that her husband, as wonderful as a person and father as he was, was to take on a different role in her life. She struggled with the decision for many years, and finally came to the conclusion that she did not want to be married to him anymore.

When my perfect pictures come into play, I move immediately, impulsively to "fix it" now. Some people with these type of pictures get immobilized, almost paralyzed and do not do anything for a long period of time. Either way, the pictures cause great suffering.

Many people thought she was crazy, because he is such a great and loving man. Other energy was thrown at her because she is a therapist, and yet can't keep her own marriage together. How was she to counsel married couples? Rebecca had perfect pictures and this was a decision that needed to be made. What held her from making the right decision for her were "perfect pictures", and what other people would think of her because she was divorced. Her choices were to keep the perfect picture, and have suffering, or break the picture and find her hearts joy. She decided to follow her heart, and she is a very happy, spiritually connected, and joyous woman.

Rebecca now has an incredible relationship with the father of her children. They moved through a divorce with love. They are very close and have developed a different level of friendship. Rebecca released her perfect pictures of what he needed to be, which gave him freedom to be who he is. Now there are no expectations on him to be a certain way. Rebecca is now filled up from God, from within, she does not look for him to grow, but because the expectations are not there, he wants to grow. When we expect to be filled up and "need" someone to feel connected to, that person can feel that energy. It feels needy and it causes the other person to back away. When you come from a place of being filled from the inside, other people will respond to that and will be there. She needed to release the perfect picture that he needed to fill her up or be a certain way, other than what he is. He is perfect, whole and complete. She is also, and therefore does not need anyone to complete her. She is already perfect.

I also experienced the perfect picture that my husband needed to be there for me to connect with me. I was looking toward him to have this emotional and spiritual connection all the time. Whenever he had things on his mind, I would feel him not being present. This is a hot button for me, as I used to perceive that my father was emotionally unavailable to me as a child. My dad was a great provider for my family. He owned his own business and worked six days a week to give us everything that we could possibly want. His definition for love as a father was, provide for your family. He learned this from his father. He was taught by his father to show love for your family, you worked hard and gave them all they could ever need. It was not his fault that he did not have the skills to provide emotionally. Many fathers in this generation didn't know how to connect spiritually with their children. They came from parents that had the philosophy that "children should be seen and not heard". My dad's own father used to tell him and his brother that very thing. This generation did not have conscious parenting magazines sitting on the coffee table. They parented like their parents did. They learned by what their parents did. Sometimes they learned what not to do. My father is very conscious about how much he drinks, because his father was an alcoholic. He did not want to be like his father in that aspect, because he saw what it did to his family. No discussions ever took place.

As a child, I took him not being available, very personally. As an adult I now know better. Dad would work all day, come home, have dinner, and then sit in front of the television for the remainder of the evening. Saturdays he would work and then my parents would go out with their friends. Sundays we would go to church and then he would spend the rest of the day watching television. As a child, I did not have much time or interaction with my father. Because of the loneliness I felt as a child, I made a decision where men where concerned. I made an agreement with myself that I will be in a relationship with a man that is always present with me. I will have a great connection with this man, always. If this man leaves me emotionally, I will leave physically. I will not settle.

Most of my relationships have led to me leaving, because the emotional connection faded away. I loved the beginning of my relationships. The men were so attentive. I knew that I was their number one priority. I would receive the love and attention that I craved when I was a child. Then the newness of the relationship would wear off. Before I could feel the men leave me emotionally, I would break off the relationship. "I will not settle".

When Mike and I started to date we had an amazing emotional, spiritual, and sexual connection. We discussed what our agreements were for our relationship. We communicated what was acceptable and not acceptable in our relationship. We talked about what would break us apart. Our first agreement was if the other person cheated, the relationship would be over. The second agreement was if he left me emotionally and spiritually, the relationship would be over. I communicated to him that I felt the connection that people have in the beginning should ever be lost. Once the newness of the relationship is over, that magic that brought the two people together should still be present. My perfect picture was based on the agreement I made with myself as a child.

This agreement had caused me to run from most of my past relationships with men.

I had a huge commitment issue, and I was married. Whenever I would feel disconnected to Mike, or felt that he was becoming emotionally unavailable, I would make threats to him that this is what will make me leave the relationship. Deepak Chopra stated in <u>The Path To Love</u> "What we fear the most is what has already happened to us in the past". This was so true for me, especially where being left emotionally was concerned. I knew Mike would never leave me physically. I truly felt that I would not want to stay in the marriage if he was not there emotionally. I don't think anyone would want that. Because of my past, and the perfect picture of what "a man being present" looked like in my own mind, no one would ever measure up. I was so hypersensitive about him being connected to me, that it was never good enough. In my mind he was unavailable just like my father was. Truth is, Mike is so present and is always there physically, spiritually, and emotionally. My friends and family comment about the way he looks at me in such adoration.

I had to realize that because of my perfect picture, a man had to treat me in a certain way, or he would never measure up. More importantly I realized that as a child, I did not know that I did not need daddy to fill me up. I did not have the knowledge or the skills to get filled from within. I did not know how to connect with the spirit inside of me. As an adult I know that I do not need anyone or anything outside of myself to fill me up. I am already perfect, whole and complete. When I am in a space of being filled up from within, I look over at my husband and I now see what other people see. I see the look in his eyes of how much he loves me. He puts me on a pedestal.

He has always in his mind put me on a pedestal, but my definition of what that looked like was different. Each person in a relationship has his or her own definition of what things mean. How one person feels they are communicating love may be completely different from how the other person communicates love. With my father as a child they thought he was showing the family love because of all that he provided for our family. As a child, my definition was if he was playing with me, he loved me. In my marriage I thought that being put on a pedestal meant being adored, admired, and complimented constantly. In Mike's mind all the things that he did to show me respect such as opening my car door, getting me a fresh towel in the morning, or showing me affection was his way of putting me on a pedestal. We both had different definitions. Now I know when he does something nice for me, and shows me respect, what that means in his mind.

8.

Being Vigilant

WHAT I HAVE WRITTEN ABOUT are my own experiences. I have read many books and understood them intellectually, but never to embody the teachings. Just as many people search for God in many different ways. People have an idea, or a "picture" of what God is or should be rather than accepting what God truly is. The bottom line, for me to heal the places where I have perfect pictures, I was to learn acceptance and non-attachment. It is a lot of hard work and needless suffering to have to have everything the way I think it should be. God's idea of what is to be is so much grander that I could ever imagine. When the little me, the ego me steps aside and I let the big me, the Real Self shine through, I am so much more abundant than I could ever imagine for myself. Some events in our lives are pleasant, others events are not. Some things are easy to enjoy. Other things are not. I do know the truth for myself is that I do not have to act crazy anymore. I do not have to go against myself. The truth for myself is that I found God. God is not some mystical thing that is out in the universe never to be touched until we die. God is everything. Everything is God. Everything that is not God is not real. I am one with God.

I know for myself that I will not find my ultimate truth through my body being a certain way, although I can create the form I want. I will not find my truth through my house, but I can create the type of house that I desire to have. I will not find my truth through my relationships or other people, but I can have wonderful, fulfilling, and joyous relationships in my life. I will not find my truth through my career, but I can desire what I want my creative expression to be. My truth is in God. My truth is where I find God in each and every moment. God is in my heart, and the heart of everyone. Jesus once said, "Where your treasure is, there will your heart be also". Meaning that if you find your deepest treasure as your material things, your heart will be there. If you find your deepest treasure as your spiritual path, your heart will be there. What you hold as most important is your treasure. Where your heart, focus, energy, and intensity are, that is what you will cultivate in your life. Honor all the things in your life that are your treasures. Treasure what God has given you in the beginning; that is your life. Take away your life, what else matters? To take in the knowledge, one needs to embody the new teachings. That takes work and it takes faith. It takes being vigilant. Whatever is in your way of joy, happiness, abundance, or whatever you desire in your life, know that you have the power to change it. You have the power to create it as you desire. Remember to be flexible, and not be attached if it should show up in a different form from what you pictured it to be. A spiritual warrior will be willing to look at those things, do the steps that need to be taken to change, and be vigilant to say "Stop", or "Cancel" whenever the old thought patterns and habit energies try to sneak back in.

My Napa Trip

I had two weeks of training with my new company in Napa, Ca. This included the weekend between the two weeks. I was excited because I was going to be in a beautiful part of the country, not to mention one of my favorite places. I had a weekend planned to have my two girlfriends come to visit me from the San Francisco Bay area. I had a great suite so we could hang out and really connect. In my mind I was going to wake up Saturday morning and workout. I had a massage scheduled for ten am. My two girlfriends were going to take two days off of work and come and spend the day and night with me.

I found out that they both had to work and that they couldn't get together until dinner. They also were not going to come to Napa and stay the night with me like a slumber party. They wanted to meet half way. I also found out one of my friends were pregnant and might not be able to make it at all. I was extremely down because my perfect day had been dramatically changed from the initial creation. I knew that it would be a great connection to see my one friend, even if it was only for a couple of hours. Being attached to the picture of what I wanted was causing me great suffering. I felt down and depressed. I called home to Mike and felt down because it wasn't going to be the way I had imagined. When I finally shifted my perception, which is not easy to do when you are in the middle of the "perfect picture" attachments, I released my need to have it my way. I had faith that God had a much better day planned for me. I had to release and surrender knowing that it would all be o.k. It was a wonderful day and completely perfect. When I detach and go with the flow, magic happens. When I am attached, suffering is there instead. It is a shift in attitude, and a shift in perception.

The weekend did turn out much better than I thought it initially would. I was able to meet both of my friends in Salcilito, on Friday night. I was introduced to a great little town on the water, just North of San Francisco. Saturday, I had my massage and then went wine tasting and spent a great day with my new friends from my company. We also went out on Saturday night and had a great time. Sunday all the girls in the group went and had spa treatments in Calistoga. It was such a great weekend. Magic happened by going with the flow and letting Spirit take over.

The Cinderella Story

My favorite movie when I was little was Cinderella. How I wanted to be a princess and find my perfect prince. Well I found my prince, but there are many days where I don't feel like Cinderella. Cinderella and her prince did not argue or have humdrum days. They lived happily ever after. The story didn't emphasize that her happiness came from within, but that there was a perfect prince out there waiting for her to save her from the hell she was living. I remember feeling like Cinderella on my wedding day. My little cousin, who was my flower girl, told me, "Christy, you look like Cinderella". It was a perfect picture that came true and I felt so beautiful. I found and married my perfect prince. When we returned home from our honeymoon I had to go back to work. I felt depressed and so let down. Cinderella did not have to go back to work, clean her house, etc. Cinderella and her prince lived happily ever after. I again suffered because it was not what I thought it should be. Many of the fairy tales and movies today all have a very similar theme. That theme is that there is one person that is going to come and save you. The stories are unrealistic. The universe is not set up that way. There is in fact the "one" that will come and save you, and make you complete, and that one is God. That God is within us. When we look outward for the one, there will be disappointment and suffering. Think about all the great love stories. I can think about my favorites, and they all end in love or tragedy. They fall in love and live happily ever after, or they fall in love and then there is some type of tragedy. I guess no one wants to see a movie about a woman that is filled from the source, from within. I guess there isn't any good drama in that. That is my point. We all get so addicted to the romance, to the drama, but the drama isn't always the healthiest. Don't get me wrong, I love being romantic with my husband. But it is in the times where I am filled up in God, coming from within me that my beloved reflects beauty, romance, and love back to me. When I look outside myself to be filled from him, or anyone or anything else, there is always disappointment, because he is not my source and supply. God is. I receive attention from other men and it is very seductive. It is very validating as a woman to be attractive to another man. There is more woman today having affairs than there are men. Why? We are looking outside of ourselves to fill us up. The only way to peace is to look within, to God, to Spirit, to our higher selves.

What the story of Cinderella did not emphasize was that Cinderella had happiness from within. Her outer circumstances reflected in the beauty that she had within herself. As we are filled within, so will be filled without. She created herself becoming a princess. No one can come and save us. We can only save ourselves. It is in the times when I am so filled up in God's love and self love that my outside reflects such beauty. In those times my husband is the most romantic and complimentary. When I go into my expectations or "perfect pictures" and look outside of myself to be filled up, I am always disappointed and there is always suffering. I have learned non-attachment, and not looking to false Gods to be the source of my good, pleasure, abundance, and personal power. For me to be so attached to what my body must look like, that is creating a false God. That is to say that when my body finally looked a certain way, my perfect body would be the source of my happiness. Many people look to money or sex as a false God. They make money the false idol, always giving money their power for happiness. When they achieve the level of money that they want, they still want more, because it truly is not the source of their happiness. It is a false God. The mind can't serve two masters. When our minds are not with God, it is somewhere else that looks as a false sense of happiness, fulfillment, good or power. Life with God is the use of the mind. God is an idea of unlimited good. God is unlimited abundance. When you are finished with your body in this lifetime will it truly be important what kind of house you lived in, or what kind of car you drove? What will matter in the end will be the love that was given and the love that was received. Our sole purpose, and soul purpose to be in these bodies is to be of service to God, to work for God. When you come with the attitude that you are here to serve, the money will be there. Think about what you do when you want a raise at work; you work harder. Since God is our source and supply of everything, including money, who is really your employer? God. So if you want to achieve more in your life and you want all of your desires to manifest, work harder for God. One of the most important spiritual laws in the universe is the law of detachment. This law states that in order to obtain anything in the physical world, you have to release your attachment to it. You can still have your desire and intention to create it, but you give up your attachment and trust that the universe will bring it together, if it is for your highest good. You must have faith and trust in Spirit, in your higher self.

In the area of my body I know what I desired to look like. I felt better inside my own skin when I was a size 2. My desire was to be a size 2, but I released my attachment to it. I set a goal for myself that my body would be a size 2. I believed with every part of my being that I could reach that goal, and that I deserved to create whatever form I wanted to. I would imagine my body as a size 2 and what that would feel like from the inside out. I took the steps toward my goal such as working out and eating well. I would do my mantras. I became aware of the beliefs that I needed to change, concerning my relationship with my body and weight. I then let it go and let God take care of the rest. When we have attachment to something it is out of fear and creation of a false

God. When we know God, and we know ourselves to be an individualized expression of God, we are able to have faith and have non-attachment. When we are detached, that is when our creative power comes through and manifests our creations. The law of detachment does not interfere with the law of intention and desire. Desire the topmost and ask God for help. Just remember, "It is God's pleasure to give you the kingdom", just don't put anything else before God.

To look for God is like a fish looking for water. Fish are surrounded and made up of water. Their whole existence is water. For us to try to search for God we are not realizing that God is in everything. We are made up of what God is. Everything is God. We are God. You and I are already perfect. The being inside each of us is a perfect creation of God. We have already reached our goals of being perfect and we did not have to do anything but tap into that truth that we are created by God, for God, and we are a perfect expression of God.

The rest of the outer circumstances such as hair, make-up, nails, weight, job, mate, etc. do your best. There is no perfection in the outside world. Once you reach the place where you thought you would want to be, you want even more because it is not yet perfect. Perfection is a moving target, never to be achieved. We have learned to live by other people's opinions, because we fear that we will not be accepted, or thought of as good enough. We have these images of what perfection is in every area of our lives, such as our bodies, careers, marriages, children, etc. We created these images in order to be accepted. Trying to be good enough for someone else will never work. You will always try to reach for someone else's approval. Self-approval is the only approval that works. If we set the standard for ourselves to be perfect, we will be disappointed because there is no perfection. We then judge and reject ourselves. When we don't fit with our own image of perfection, we truly feel that we are not good enough. So what can we do to free ourselves from the illusion of perfection? How do we continue to strive for the best in life without placing too high of expectations on others or ourselves? We do our best.

If you are always doing your best, you can't judge yourself. If you know at the end of the day that you gave all you have, you can't feel guilt, blame, or self-hatred. If you want to loose weight, and you did everything on your plan for the day, and you did your best, that is all you can do. If you try to do more than your best, it is a waste of energy and will lead to suffering. When you do the best that you can do, you will learn self-acceptance.

When you do your best, understand that you are human, and not perfect. If we were perfect, we would be flying with wings on our backs. One day you may give your best and it may be less than you gave the day before. Only you can answer the question, "Did I do my best?"

With this new way of challenging yourself to push yourself to do your best and be your best, you will be able to release perfect pictures and know you gave it your all. By always doing your best you will continue to grow and evolve and the achievements in your life will be amazing. Don't compare yourself with anyone else. In every moment do your best. Go for greatness. Do your best and know that who you are is already perfect.

AND SO IT IS!

9.

Treatments for every day
Of the week

Sunday:

God is the unlimited abundance and happiness in the universe. Scarcity and lack do not exist in God's universe. There is only the acceptance of love, abundance, joy, peace, and happiness available to each and every person. God does not withhold anything from anyone. I am one with this God. I am abundant, for I live in an abundant universe. I am a co-creator with God. I now accept for myself unlimited abundance. I open my heart and my mind to accept unlimited good into my consciousness. I release any fears, doubts, or lack thoughts that do not serve me, or the universe. I accept only deep love and boundless happiness for myself, and others. I am grateful for this knowing and that I am an individualized expression of God. I am grateful for my life and for all of my blessings. I release this treatment, now choosing abundance for myself, and my life.

And So It Is.

Monday

Beloved Presence, Sweet Loving Spirit, thank you for my life. This one Spirit is the creative and loving Being of all that is. This spirit is unlimited courage and power that is available to every being.

I am one with this sweet, powerful spirit. I am apart of this spirit. My mind, body, and soul are made up of this one being. I now choose to accept myself the way I am, without judgment. I know that I am already perfect and complete. I clean my mind of any negative thought patterns and self-hatred, so that I can live peacefully.

Thank you for the opportunity to change my thoughts and change my life to create an even more beautiful existence. I release this treatment in total trust and faith,

And So It Is!

Tuesday

Divine knowledge is flowing in, around, and through me directing everything I do. My mind, body, and affairs reflect the completeness and abundance of the Universe.

Infinite Mind provides all the supply I can use to achieve my wholeness. It flows lavishly in the form of wonderful ideas, creative expression, and inspiration. I participate fully and joyously in life, and I am open to receive in return. I am worthy of all the spiritual and material riches that are available in the universe. Anything within me that stands to block the flow of this Truth is released and transformed into a new and greater truth. I love, appreciate, and use God's abundance wisely and in harmony with the Universe. I acknowledge God as the only source and substance that there is. I release this treatment with love,

And So It Is!

Wednesday

I forgive all those whom I have been holding in my mind, as people who have hurt me in some way. Because of the law "As you sow, so shall you reap," I take full responsibility for what has happened in, around, and to me. I start today fresh and new as the person that I desire to be with total faith in my potential and God. I know the truth of me and the truth of what is God. I give up any place in my mind that I hold resentment, lamentation, anger, or jealousy. I claim all the abundance and prosperity that is my birthright. I am a child of God, perfect and complete. I celebrate this knowing as my truth. I am grateful, for every good in my life. I release this treatment knowing it is so,

And So It Is!

Thursday

There is only One Life-the Life of Spirit. I live in unity with all that is, recognizing its presence in everyone and everything. The full power and presence of God is available to me right now. I now choose for myself the Divine attributes of wisdom, strength, prosperity, joy, health, and harmony. Knowing I am made in the image and likeness of God, I understand it works for me by working through me. Right here and right now I embody new agreements in my life. I choose to be impeccable with my word, for my word creates my reality. I no longer take what other people say, do, think, or feel personally. In not taking things personally I increase my personal power. I never make assumptions, for I ask questions when I am unclear. I only perceive love and release the thoughts of fear and lack. I always do my best, knowing that when I do my best I can't judge myself. I am alive in Spirit, and Spirit is alive in me. As I embody these new agreements, I release the old agreements that no longer serve me, or the planet. I am so grateful for my life and awakening to new consciousness. I release this treatment with all that no longer serves me.

And So It Is!

Friday

Today my faith in God and my good fortune is increasing. Knowing that God is my source and supply, there is no need to focus on doubt or fear. I choose total faith and release any place that I may have doubt. For I know that doubt creates despair, and I do not wish to create that in my life. I choose to create absolute abundance, happiness, health, prosperity, and consciousness in my life. I am one with the Creator, as a Co-Creator with this amazing Spirit. I accept today, manifestation of my unlimited good and abundance. I know as my truth that Infinite Spirit is flowing through my mind, and is enriching and guiding me to think, speak, and do that which is for my best at all times. That which is not for my highest good fades from my life, and I no longer desire it. Thank you for this knowledge of my truth. As I embody it, it becomes my life. I accept it, and let it be so.

And So It Is!

Saturday

With God as my source and supply, my protector and maintainer, I know that there is nothing to ever worry about ever again. God is the unlimited source of confidence, success, happiness, and abundance available to me now and always. I am totally accepting of the success and abundance that is available to me. My heart is filled with gratitude for this knowing and the many blessing I receive each day in my life. My self-love and self-approval brings love and approval to others and the world. Ideas of self-doubt, self-destruction, or self-worthlessness have no foundation for power and no possibility for demonstration in my life. I am committed to loving the Infinite Power of the Universe by loving its expression as me. I go about my day loving and approving of myself, because I am wonderful. I am already perfect, whole and complete.

And So It Is!

References:

Webster's Ninth New Collegiate Dictionary, 1987

Hanh, T. N. (2001). <u>Anger</u>. New York, N.Y.: Penguin Putnam Inc.

Whittaker, T.C. (1979). <u>What You Think Of Me Is None Of My Business.</u> New York, N.Y.: Penguin Putnam Inc.

Whittaker, T.C. (2000). <u>21 Days To Personal Riches & Generating Wealth Workbook.</u>

Chopra, D. (1994). <u>The Seven Spiritual Laws of Success.</u> San Rafael, CA.: Amber-Allen Publishing and New World Library

Ruiz, D. M (1997). <u>The Four Agreements.</u> San Rafael, CA.: Amber-Allen Publishing, Inc.

Music Index, 2003

Pink (2002). Don't Let Me Get Me. Arista Records

Chopra, D. (1997). <u>The Path To Love.</u> New York, N.Y.: Three Rivers Press

<u>The New Testament of Our Lord and Savior Jesus Christ.</u> Nashville, TN, 1985. National Publishing Company.

Williamson, M. (1990). Lecture tapes on the Course in Miracles. New York, N.Y.: Harper Audio a division of Harper-Collins Publishers, Inc.

LuminEssence Productions. Ashland, OR. (541) 770-6700. www.orindaben.com

Lockhart, A. (1994). <u>Positive Charges.</u> Richmond, VA.: Zander Press

Dyer, W. (1991). <u>Your Erroneous Zones.</u> New York, N.Y.: Harper Collins Publishers, Inc.

Robbins, A. (2001). <u>Get The Edge.</u> San Diego, CA.: Robbins Research International, Inc. (800)898-8669

Printed in the United States
1299200004B/220-228